The Official FA Guide for
Football Parents

LEARNING

The Official FA Guide for
Football Parents

Les Howie

Hodder & Stoughton

A MEMBER OF THE HODDER HEADLINE GROUP

For order enquiries: please contact Bookpoint Ltd, 130 Milton Park, Abingdon, Oxon
OX14 4SB. Telephone: +44 (0) 1235 827720. Fax: +44 (0) 1235 400454. Lines are open
from 09.00–18.00, Monday to Saturday, with a 24-hour message-answering service.
Details about our titles and how to order are available at www.madaboutbooks.com

British Library Cataloguing in Publication Data:
a catalogue record for this title is available from the British Library.

ISBN 0 340 816023

First Published 2004
Impression number   10 9 8 7 6 5 4 3 2 1
Year   2007 2006 2005 2004

Managing Editor: Jonathan Wilson, FA Learning

Typeset by Servis Filmsetting Ltd, Manchester.
Printed in Great Britain for Hodder & Stoughton Educational, a division of Hodder
Headline Plc, 338 Euston Road, London NW1 3BH by Cox & Wyman, Reading, Berkshire.

Hodder Headline's policy is to use papers that are natural, renewable and recyclable
products and made from wood grown in sustainable forests. The logging and
manufacturing processes are expected to conform to the environmental regulations of the
country of origin.

Contents

LEARNING

Dedication

Writing this book has brought back many happy memories, and made me realize how lucky I was to have such a positive introduction to this great game. I would like to dedicate this book to my Dad, my Grandad and my Uncle Mac, who all helped introduce me to the game.

Looking forward, I also want to dedicate this book to my children, Becky, Katie and Tom, who are enabling me to see it from the other side of the fence, and giving me the great privilege of introducing them to the game, and being a Football Parent.

Philosophy of the guides

The aim of these **Official FA Guides** is to reach the millions of people who participate in football or who are involved in the game in other ways – at any level.

Each book aims to increase your awareness and understanding of association football and in this understanding to enhance, increase, improve and extend your involvement in the world's greatest game.

These books are designed to be interactive and encourage you to apply what you read and to help you to translate this knowledge into practical skills and ability. Specific features occur throughout this book to assist this process:

■ Tasks will appear in this form and will make you think about what you have just learned and how you will apply it in a practical way.

Best Practice The Best Practice feature will give you an example of a good or ideal way of doing things – this could be on or off the pitch.

Quote

'Quotes throughout will pass on useful knowledge or insight or encourage you to consider a certain aspect of your skills or responsibilities.'

Statistic

The statistics included will often surprise and will certainly increase your knowledge of the game.

Summary

- **The summaries at the end of each chapter will recap on its contents and help you to consolidate your knowledge and understanding.**

You can read this guide in any way you choose and prefer to do so – at home, on the pitch, in its entirety, or to dip in for particular advice. Whatever way you use it, we hope it increases your ability, your knowledge, your involvement, and most importantly your enjoyment and passion to **be a part of the game**.

Introduction

| Quote | 'We have all watched it. The majority of us will have played it. Some of us will have read about it. And a select few will have written and commentated on it.' |

Football is known as the 'people's game' because it is one of the few aspects of a person's life that has the ability to bring people together

irrespective of their sex, age, religion or race. It is the world's most popular sport by far, has been so for over 100 years and the game is now attracting more spectators and participants than ever before. Football is played all over the world and can be described as a truly global language.

Even with wall-to-wall media coverage and all the experience you will probably have of the game, by reading this book you will be embarking on a new critical role in the game. You are about to enter the world of the football parent.

The football parent

Quote | 'The role of a football parent is arguably the most important in the game.'

Your job as a football parent is to support, guide and develop a lifelong love and passion of this great sport in your child.

This book sets out to provide you with practical advice, ideas and support that will help you not only develop your child's interests in the game, but will also assist in helping you to get more enjoyment from football.

Generally the greatest influence in a child's life is their parent and for the majority of today's adult football supporters their passion for the game will have come from their parents. If your child's interest in the game starts to develop then it is your duty to support and encourage this, much in the same way as if your child develops an interest in any other sport or activity.

At the start we should make it clear that the most important aspect of being a football parent is not whether you have 100 caps for your country or that you watch every live game on television, it is about support, encouragement and helping your child develop their love of the game. For some parents this will be from the sidelines, for others it will involve washing the team kit, while others may even learn how to coach, but whatever your role we are sure that this will be a challenging and exciting one.

As a parent of three young children I have rediscovered some of the key principles of the game through the time I've spent introducing my children to football. I hope that in this book I can pass on some of my experience and knowledge gained through my role in The FA, and more importantly as a football parent.

Roles of the football parent

You may have been a player, a coach, a referee or a fan, but you are now a football parent, which means you may also become the following:

- Coach,
- Mentor,
- Taxi service,
- Shoulder to cry on when it all goes wrong,
- Cheerleader,
- Kit washer,
- First aider,
- Orange cutter-upper,
- Diplomat,
- Role model,
- Ball fetcher,
- Water carrier,
- Fan,
- Constructive critic.

▨ Look at the jobs listed on page xiii and think about the ways in which you could help because at some point you may be asked to lend a hand.

Quote	'The role of a football parent can be time consuming, challenging, diverse and not always fully appreciated, but at the same time it can also be fantastically rewarding.'

So let's enter the world of the football parent!

Chapter 1

Sharing an interest

THIS CHAPTER WILL:

- Look at the positive reasons for your child to be involved in football.
- Highlight the reasons why children want to play.
- Consider the potential influences that could affect participation.

I can still remember going with my granddad to watch my local club Newcastle United play when I was seven. It was an end-of-season game on a wet Wednesday night and Newcastle United were playing Everton. We were going as a treat, as my granddad had promised me for what had seemed like ages and finally he had saved up the money so we could afford to sit in the 'new stand'.

The final score was 0-0 but the overriding memory was of the amazing atmosphere, the camaraderie between the Newcastle fans and the smell at the ground, which I later discovered was the smell of the hops at the brewery that was opposite St James' Park.

St James' Park as it looks today

Over the next 15 years I went to watch football with my dad, and as I got older with my friends. Saturdays always felt like a privilege – sharing the same stadia with some of the finest players to wear the famous black and white shirts of the 'magpies'. I went through all manner of emotional ups and downs watching Newcastle United. I saw great players like Super Mac (Malcolm McDonald), Beardsley, Waddle, Gascoigne as well as cup finals at Wembley, Kevin Keegan's debut, promotion and of course relegation.

Quote | 'People remember their first football match like their first kiss – for many it's like a rite of passage that will never be forgotten.'

My enjoyment of football was encouraged by my family but it wasn't simply about watching the game. It was also about playing football in the street, at school, in PE lessons, in the school team, in the playground or in the back garden.

Best Practice Unfortunately times have changed over the last 30 years and now parents must be more vigilant than ever before. Always make sure that you know exactly where your child is going to play football, have an agreed time for their return, always make sure that they are not alone. If possible have an adult either supervise the game or be close by, just in case.

Today, 30 years later, I've started to introduce my children to live games and I still get that same buzz and excitement as I did when I was growing up. I just hope that I can pass this enthusiasm onto the children and that they get as much enjoyment from the game as I do.

The point of sharing my personal experiences with you is that in this chapter we are going to look at sharing and developing interest in the game and how we might do this. We will also look at some of the influences that might affect your child's participation and we will discuss the difference between football for adults and children and what this means.

▓ Think about the first game you went to watch. What was it like and what do you remember about it?

Developing interest

Perhaps a good starting point is to take your child to a football match. It doesn't have to be a professional game – I went to watch games on the field at the end of my street where the local amateur team, Lindisfarme played in the Northern Alliance League.

Best Practice Football is played at all levels, from the local park to huge all-seater stadia in front of tens of thousands of adoring fans. To make sure that your child gets a good understanding of the different types of football that take place, take them to a few local matches where the skill levels might not be quite so high but the experience of being so close to the play makes the game just as exciting.

Watching football on TV

This is going to make me sound old, but when I was growing up, there were usually only two live games on television in England per season: The FA Cup Final and England vs. Scotland. From time to time there was also a schoolboy international or England World Cup qualifier and every four years the World Cup, but unfortunately England failed to qualify for any of the World Cups that took place when I was a child!

Today football and television go hand in hand – hundreds of matches are shown live and are repeated almost every day of the week. Whether you want to watch the very best in the world on the international stage or a non-league side there is a good chance a television station will be covering the game. The increased exposure of football on television gives families lots of opportunities to watch the game together. However, be prepared for lots of questions because this is how your child will learn about the game.

Statistic

Over **8 million** households now have access to satellite television in the UK.

Talking

Spend time with your child discussing the game:

- 'That was a good game, what do you think?'
- 'Do you think that was a free kick?'
- 'Who do you think was the best player on the pitch?'
- 'Do you think the goalkeeper should have saved that goal?'

By talking to your child it will not only help your child's football knowledge and understanding of the game, but also their social and communication skills.

Watch a game (either live at the ground or on television) and then spend some time discussing the match.

Why do children play football?

In a recent survey carried out by The FA, the following reasons were provided to explain why children play football:

- **To be with friends.**
- **To improve their skills.**
- **The excitement of the competition.**
- **To be part of a team.**
- **To play the game.**
- **To become a professional.**
- **As a result of encouragement from parents (although this encouragement can go too far and become a pressure on the child).**
- **Because it's fun!**

■   Think about the most important reasons why you would want your child to play football and what you would want them to gain from the experience.

Other reasons why children might play football could be:

- **It's easy to set up – all you need is a ball and some clothes to mark out goalposts.**

- It's simple – there are only 17 rules and most people don't know them all, yet it doesn't stop people from playing and having fun. In the street or on the field you can even make up your own rules.

- You need little personal equipment – you don't need a set of clubs, a bat, a racquet or lots of padding (except your shin guards). This also makes football a relatively cheap sport to play. You can improvise even if you don't have a ball – this doesn't usually stop school children from finding something else that they can use instead!

What are the benefits of football to children?

Football provides the child with many benefits:

1   Provides healthy activity,

2   Encourages fitness and exercise,

3   Builds confidence,

4   Helps the child to socialize,

5   Develops self-discipline,

6   Encourages a sense of self-respect and respect for others,

7   Develops teamwork and co-operation,

8   Helps the child to handle success and failure,

9   Helps to develop communication skills,

10 Provides a challenge,

11 Enables the child to make new friends,

12 Encourages parental involvement.

▨   Can you think of any other benefits that football provides for your child?

Influences on a child's participation

Many factors can influence a child's participation in football – here are
some of the most common:

Television can dominate a child's free time, so
make sure there's always time for football.

Food plays a key part in successful participation
in football, so please try to help with a balanced
diet. I'm not saying no crisps, chocolate or
burgers, but try to achieve a balanced diet,
which provides the child with the energy to take
part in the game.

We all need sleep and children usually need
more than adults, so please ensure that children
go to bed at an appropriate time. If they don't
their performance and enjoyment of the game
will be affected.

Being part of a club means getting the child to
training and to games. Sometimes you won't be
available because of work commitments – this
can't be helped but be aware of them. For
example, can a friend take or bring back your
child from training?

Perhaps the school that your child attends doesn't play football, or your child may be expected to play other sports. There may be no teacher support for the game or homework may make participating in football problematic.

Spare time activities

Table 1 highlights exactly what children of different ages enjoy doing in their spare time. As you can see, at all ages football remains pretty high on the list, although as the child gets older the game's popularity does start to reduce a little as physical activity becomes less of a priority.

Table 1

	7–9 Boys	7–9 Girls	10–12 Boys	10–12 Girls	13–15 Boys	13–15 Girls
Listening to music	47/81		60/85		77/96	
Shopping for clothes	12/61		18/75		29/90	
Playing football	**91/48**		**86/49**		**81/33**	
Hanging around with friends	76/80		80/89		83/89	
Watching TV	85/81		73/78		80/79	
Going to the cinema	57/64		58/66		56/78	
Playing solo sports	n/a		33/18		36/23	
Computer games	82/65		80/52		81/39	
Playing team sports	58/37		56/38		50/35	
Swimming	67/81		58/76		49/57	
Watching football on TV	**71/29**		**70/34**		**70/34**	
The internet	29/36		45/43		58/62	
Reading	36/59		27/48		22/40	

Statistic

In England over **250,000** children play organized Mini Soccer.

Many parents will have played or watched football as adults but we must remember that there are differences between the game adults play and the one that children enjoy:

- The playing area is usually smaller.
- Equipment is adapted (particularly in Mini Soccer).
- Playing periods will be shorter.
- Players should be encouraged to try different positions.
- In Mini Soccer (The FA's recommended game for children under ten) team numbers are smaller so that children feel more involved and get more touches of the ball.

What sort of football programme do you want for your child?

We will discuss this in more detail in Chapter 3, but to help you begin to think about this issue, rank the following statements in order 1–10 (1 = most important, 10 = least important).

- Children should be encouraged, but not forced to take part in football.
- It should be win at all costs.
- Football should be promoted equally for boys and girls.
- Children should try a variety of activities.
- Competitions should be appropriately organized.
- The needs of the child must come first.
- Football should be fun.
- The adult game should be adapted to suit children.
- All children should be catered for.
- Everyone should get a game.

Take a few minutes to complete the above task so that you can start to look at the different issues and what you feel is most important.

LEARNING

Summary

- **Reflect on your own football experiences.**

- **Attend games with your child.**

- **Watch games together on TV and encourage lots of questions.**

- **Children play for lots of reasons, but always for fun.**

- **Football provides many benefits for the child.**

- **Be aware of outside influences and manage these as part of a balanced life.**

- **Remember that children are not 'mini-adults'.**

- **Decide what sort of football programme you and your child wish to participate in.**

Self testers

1 What are the potential influences on a child's participation in football?

2 List as many reasons as you can as to why children play football.

3 What are the benefits of children playing football?

Action plan

If your child has shown an interest in the game, spend time talking to them about their reasons for being involved in football, take them to a game and point out the positive things that happen during a match such as teamwork, scoring a goal and celebrating together.

LEARNING

Chapter 2

The garden coach

THIS CHAPTER WILL:
- Help you to get started as a football parent.
- Look at the concept of physical literacy and the principles of long-term athlete development.
- Introduce you to a variety of garden games.
- Show you how to use FA Soccer Star.

If you only remember one thing from this book remember this: **let the game be the teacher**.

When did you first kick a ball and start playing football?

Top tips for getting started

- You're not Sven Goran Eriksson, Fabio Cappello or Alex Ferguson, so don't take the game too seriously and remember to have fun.

- Use the appropriate size football for the age of your child. You want to give them the best start possible and using the right equipment will help.

- Don't keep stopping your child when you're in the middle of a practice or game. Give them the ball and let them kick it. Football is all about being creative and being able to experiment and practise skills that you can then take onto the field when playing in a game. Johan Cryuff didn't just invent his famous turn on the spot in front of thousands of people in the World Cup, it was only thanks to hours of practice and no doubt getting it wrong a few times too. So let your child have fun.

Quote | 'No matter what your age, football is about having fun; otherwise what is the point in playing at all?'

- Don't keep stopping to correct faults. I had a long debate with a parent who was worried that his child sometimes 'toe punted' the ball. Even after explaining that one of Ronaldo's goals in the

2002 World Cup Final was a 'toe punt', the parent still wouldn't accept that in the right circumstances a 'toe punt' can be considered a skill.

Quote | 'Remember that 'skill' means doing the right technique at the right time.'

- Don't be technical. As we have said previously, let your child have fun and learn the game naturally without too much technical coaching from the patio.

- Encourage your child to try new things. For example, can they kick the ball with different parts of the foot such as their heel, instep or their toes? And what about their less preferred foot?

- Praise any effort that your child makes and always be positive. Make sure that you encourage your child to keep trying because practice makes perfect, and if not perfect at the very least they will improve.

- Praise your child when he or she has done well.

- Let your child have fun – this way he or she will want to play again and again.

▨ Think of a player you like – why do you like him/her, what does he/she do well? Now ask your child to do the same.

Physical literacy and principles of long-term athlete development

Now we have all heard on the news the concerns in education of the need to develop a child's literacy skills. Well, one of the biggest concerns in sport is the lack of physical literacy in children today. Physical literacy is about being able to:

- Skip,
- Jog,

- **Run,**
- **Catch,**
- **Throw,**
- **Strike an object,**
- **Balance,**
- **Co-ordination/agility.**

Before you can be a footballer, you need to be able to perform most of the key skills of physical literacy listed above. That is why it is important that we encourage children to have a healthy and active life style and try to learn these skills by participating in active games rather than just playing computer games. Although interest in many sports has never been greater, parents play a crucial role in capitalizing on this interest by getting out in the garden with their child and trying to recreate the skills they see on television or on a computer game.

Here are some simple activities you can do in the garden or local park to develop your child's physical literacy:

- Skipping – an old favourite, all you need is some rope and anyone who thinks skipping is just for girls hasn't seen boxers train!
- Walking/Jogging/Running – do you always really need to take the car, or could you walk or jog instead?
- Catching and throwing games – children of any age can take part in these, and they really help with hand-eye co-ordination.

■ Use the list of physical literacy attributes on pages 17–18 and the games suggested above as a guide and think of additional games that you could play with your child to improve these skills.

Games for the garden

In the garden or at the local recreation ground you can set up the following simple football activity that involves running:

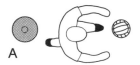

1   Jog with the ball from A to B.
2   Leave the ball and jog to C.
3   Go round C and sprint back to B.
4   At B get the ball and jog back to A.

As an alternative you could use a sideways skip instead of jogging.

This simple exercise introduces:

- **Running with the ball,**
- **Jogging,**
- **Changing speed,**
- **Skipping.**

For the next activity you will need to set out a square – 5 m × 5 m is the ideal size.

Anfield   St James' Park

Old Trafford   Wembley

1 **A player jogs around the middle with a ball, keeping it under control.**

2 **Give a ground name to each corner. Shout out a ground name and the player must leave the ball and run to that corner.**

3 **Shout 'ground tour' and the player must touch all four corners.**

You could progress this activity by getting the players to take the ball with them to each corner rather than simply running.

The exercise introduces:

- **Ball familiarity,**
- **Running,**

- Changing direction,
- Running with the ball.

Catch

1 Ask your child to throw the ball up in the air and catch it.

2 As your child becomes more confident ask him/her to throw the ball higher.

3 Throw the ball against the wall and catch it on return.

4 You throw for the child to catch.

5 If there are three of you set up a triangle for throwing and catching or play one in the middle, so that A must throw the ball to C, if B catches the ball then A goes in the middle, if C doesn't catch the ball then C goes in the middle.

A variation on this is to get your child to stand 5 m away from the wall, and you stand behind and throw the ball against the wall. Your child then tries to catch, and as they get more successful they move closer to the wall. This improves reaction times and ability to catch the ball.

These activities, as well as improving catching skills, also help to develop your child's ability to throw.

Strike

Practise the skill of striking a ball by encouraging your child to strike a ball with a bat. Here are a few ideas to help practise this skill.

1 **Bounce a ball on a tennis racquet (keep ups).**
2 **Use the racquet to bounce the ball on the ground.**
3 **Use the racquet for keep ups against the wall.**

I can hear you asking, 'what has this got to do with football?' Well, this actually helps to develop hand-eye co-ordination, balance and reflex – all important attributes of a footballer.

All of these activities can be done in a confined space, for example, your garden or driveway and will assist in improving your child's physical literacy.

Improving physical literacy

■ Think of a game you can do in a small area that will help your child's physical literacy.

The following guidelines should help you to improve your child's physical literacy:

• **You should train/practise three times each week for every game you play. This training can include:**
  • **Formal club training nights,**
  • **School PE,**
  • **Playing in the garden,**
  • **Self-practice.**
• **The need to avoid overplay. This is of particular importance for elite performers (see overuse in Chapter 9) and young participants whose bodies are still developing and so can be more susceptible to injury.**

Best Practice Parents need to look at the whole range of sporting activities that their child plays when trying to avoid overplay. For many children football will be just one of a range of sports and so when planning a child's schedule take in to account all the sports they are involved in and ensure that they receive adequate rest periods to allow their developing bodies to rest and recuperate.

- Footballers should have at least 10,000 touches of the ball before they are 16 so that they are comfortable with the ball, and have developed confidence and skill. In an average youth game some players may get less than ten touches of the ball. Whilst in training, where everyone should have a ball, the number of touches can reach the hundreds. This shows you the importance of training and practising.

Quote | 'Mini Soccer was developed to allow children to play on smaller pitches in smaller teams so that they get more involved and have more touches of the ball.'

- In developing young players the emphasis should be on development and improvement and should not be results driven.

Garden games

Here are some games to try in the garden or at the local park.

Ball control

1 Pass the ball to the child who controls the ball and passes it back.

2 As the child becomes more confident use one-touch passing.

3 Introduce movement by using three cones.

4 On passing the ball back, the child must run to touch cone C, then back to B and repeat.

You

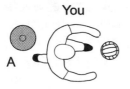

A

Child

B

C

5   As the child becomes more confident you can progress by
    serving the ball gently at thigh height. The child controls the
    ball and passes it back.

6   The next progression is to throw the ball so the child can volley
    back to you.

7   As the child becomes confident with the control, introduce
    movement by asking them to control the ball, run with the ball
    to cone C, turn, run back to cone B and pass back to you.

Creating space

1   Face your child. Give the ball to your child.

2   Run towards each other with your child kicking the ball on the
    ground. When close your child shouts 'take' and you take the
    ball.

3   Repeat, but this time your child takes the ball from you.

4   To progress instead of shouting 'take' and the other person taking
    the ball, this time the person with the ball puts their foot on it as
    they meet the other person, who then takes the ball. Repeat this
    many times to ensure each person has lots of turns at it.

Shooting

1   First, set up a goal. This could be with cones, by making marks
    on a wall or even using some jumpers for goalposts.

2   Get your child to shoot at the goal. You can set them targets, for example:

- Bottom left,
- Top right,
- Middle of goal.

3   Get them to shoot from different angles – some from the left, some from the right, some from the centre.

4   Increase the distance between your child and the goalposts as far as their confidence and strength will allow.

5   Remember, try both feet and try different parts of the foot – instep and laces.

Running with the ball

1   Get your child to run around a defined area, with the ball at their feet.

2   Shout by using the following codes to get them to do different tasks:

- 1 = stop with foot on ball.
- 2 = try a turn.
- 3 = run with the ball.
- 4 = five toe taps with alternate feet.

3   As the child gets more competent introduce obstacles into the area for them to avoid, such as cones or clothing.

Heading

Next time you watch a children's game count how many headers you see.

There are lots of reasons why you won't see many headers from children. This is generally because:

- Children can't cross the ball yet.
- They can't judge the speed, so they miss the header.
- They're afraid of heading the ball.

Best Practice Don't introduce heading too early, and when you do, build up the exercises slowly to encourage the child and increase their confidence.

Use the following list of practices for guidance:

1 Get the child to head the ball in their hands.

2 Ask the child to throw the ball up gently and head it.

3 As the child becomes more confident ask him/her to throw the ball a bit higher.

4 Another way to encourage heading is to start with a balloon or soft ball (sponge ball).

5 When your child is confident, you may then move onto gently serving the ball from a short distance.

6 As the strength and confidence develops you can move further away from your child to throw the ball.

■   Think about the games you enjoyed as a child – how can you introduce these games to your children?

FA Soccer Star

The FA has produced an interactive website that provides players, coaches and parents with a series of skills tests. Visit **www.TheFA. com**/FALearning to look at the games then go outside and put them into practice.

The games are designed for children aged 6–16 and are fun and engaging. The games also challenge children to think about some of the simple issues covered within the game in an educational context. The message of the games is clear – football should be inclusive and fun and kids are able to challenge their friends and parents. As well as improving your child's skills, it's a chance to profile their strengths and weaknesses.

Benefits of the Soccer Star tests include:

* **Tests and certificates that are designed to reward achievement.**
* **The advocacy of the benefits of practice to improve scores. The provision of recommended learning programmes with suitable practices for young players.**
* **The opportunity to download the free Soccer Star Challenge certificates.**

Statistic

Since its launch in 1998 over **20,000** coaches from over 120 countries have used Soccer Star.

■   Visit **www.TheFA.com**/FALearning with your child, register with FA Learning and then enrol on Soccer Star and choose two activities to do together to get you started.

Summary

- **Let the game be the teacher.**

- **Don't keep stopping the activity, let them play and practice.**

- **Encourage your child to try new things.**

- **Introduce activities that help develop your child's physical literacy.**

- **Think about what garden games you can introduce your child to.**

- **Next time you're at a game or watching on TV, with your child, get them to choose a skill they see a player do, then try to master it in the garden.**

Self testers

1 What are the key elements of children's physical literacy?
2 How many touches of a ball should footballers have before they are 16?
3 What are the main reasons why children often don't head the ball?

Action plan

Look at the aspects of the game that your child enjoys the most and use the practice exercises and tasks to enhance these aspects. Look at any problem areas and try to use relevant tasks in this chapter to improve these in a fun, encouraging environment.

Chapter 3

Finding the right club or football camp programme

THIS CHAPTER WILL:
- Help you decide on the most suitable programme for your child.
- Give advice on what to look for in a club/football camp.
- Suggest the questions that you should ask when taking your child to a new football camp/club.

You've just bought a new car. It's your pride and joy and sits in your drive. Suddenly there is a knock at your door. Standing in front of you is a complete stranger. He asks if he can borrow your car for two hours on a Tuesday evening and every Sunday morning – what's your answer?

I can bet it wouldn't be yes and even if it were, you would ask lots of questions. Unfortunately whilst many people would be very careful about who they would allow to borrow their car, many aren't always so careful when lending their real pride and joy – their children!

Belonging to an affiliated football club and participating in football programmes, coaching courses and holiday camps are becoming an increasingly popular way for children to spend their free time and school holidays. But do parents really consider the different options carefully, in terms of which would be the best for their child?

Quote | 'Parents must think carefully before deciding which club their child will play for.'

There is a lot for parents to consider before deciding where to send their child. Aspects such as the experience and qualifications of the coaches, the facilities, their location, the safety of their child, cost and value for money all need to be taken into account and in this chapter we aim to provide advice, hints and tips that parents should read before agreeing to send their child to any football programme.

Finding the right club or programme

Statistic
In England there are now over **300,000** boys playing for over **20,000** affiliated teams.

Remember that most children play football to be with friends, to improve their skills and because it's fun.

Visit the clubs in your area in order to find the right one that suits your child.

Not all skills are learned on the training ground, some can be picked up in more informal settings, so get involved and help your child in the garden!

It is important that you support your child, so make sure that when you can, you go to watch him/her play.

Offer your expertise to the club if you want to get involved – whatever your profession, it is likely you'll be able to help out in some way.

Appropriate equipment is important, but when your child demands the latest and most expensive kit remind them that skilful players do not score great goals just because of the boots they wear.

Remember that most children play football to be with friends, to improve their skills and because it's fun.

Visit the clubs in your area in order to find the right one that suits your child.

Not all skills are learned on the training ground, some can be picked up in more informal settings, so get involved and help your child in the garden!

It is important that you support your child, so make sure that when you can, you go to watch him/her play.

Offer your expertise to the club if you want to get involved – whatever your profession, it is likely you'll be able to help out in some way.

Appropriate equipment is important, but when your child demands the latest and most expensive kit remind them that skilful players do not score great goals just because of the boots they wear.

Before you begin to look around for a suitable club or programme you and your child need to ask yourselves some questions:

• What level of commitment is expected in terms of frequency of training and matches?

• Which nights are for training and when are games played? If training is on a Tuesday and you are not available you will need to think again.

• How far are you willing to travel? Some clubs have fixtures that involve over one hour's travelling time.

• What is the cost involved? Some programmes and clubs are more expensive than others. Remember the most expensive aren't necessarily the best.

• What do you want your child to achieve? Is it just about winning?

• What is the best learning environment for your child? Do you want a fun 'everyone plays' philosophy, or a very competitive environment?

▓   Answer the questions above to give you a better idea about the factors that are important to you and list your answers in order of priority.

The next step in finding the right club/programme

Now we have a good idea about the kind of club/football camp we are looking for, the next step is to find it! Here are some top tips:

• Contact your local County Football Association or local organization. They will be able to provide you with a list of clubs and programmes being offered in your area.

• Ask other parents and get their feedback.

• Ask other children such as your child's friends.

• Ask at school as many clubs have, over a number of years, developed excellent relationships with their local school.

- Research clubs and programme providers by looking in the local press, on the internet and even in the Yellow Pages.

▓ List five questions you would ask another parent when trying to find a club/football camp.

Before you visit

You have your list of requirements, you've asked around and now you've decided on the best club or programme for your child.

Before you make contact or visit find out if the club has a website. If it does, visit it as the website can give you so much information, such as:

- How old the club is – if it has been around for a number of years this tells you it is probably reliable and is sustainable.
- Its achievements – if it lists lots of cup and league successes, then it may be that a great deal of emphasis is placed on winning.
- Its philosophy.
- A list of officials – so you know who you will be dealing with.

Best Practice Don't just visit one website – check out a few to get a feel of the market. Look at what clubs have to offer and make sure that you agree with their philosophy in terms of how the game is played (for example, is it just about winning or about fun, enjoyment and making sure everyone gets a game?).

The first visit

Once you have done your research and chosen your club or programme it's time to make contact and visit for the first time. On the first visit here are some tips on what to look out for:

- Is there a welcoming atmosphere?
- Are there lots of happy, smiling faces, particularly the children?
- Are other parents present and are they watching or are they kept away from the children?
- Is there a good coach to player ratio? Generally this should be two coaches per squad with a maximum 1:16 ratio.

Best Practice Don't forget to take your child with you when you visit the team for the first time! Ultimately your child will need to be central in the decision-making process and if he/she doesn't like the club or teammates and doesn't feel comfortable, then the philosophy of the club will be irrelevant. The decision needs to be one that allows both the parent and the child to be happy and confident that the child will have an enjoyable, fun experience.

Observation won't tell you everything so here are some questions that you may find useful:

- When and where is training? Is this convenient to you and your child?

- When and where does the club play and how do the players get there?

- How much does it cost? Ask about all costs including membership, training and match fees and kit costs.

- Does the club follow The Football Association child protection procedures? This should be a very definite yes! You can check The FA policy on **www.TheFA.com**.

- What child protection training have the staff had?

- Does the club have a child protection/welfare contact person? If yes who is it?

- How does the club recruit its coaches and staff? They should get coaches and staff to complete forms, carry out interviews and obtain references. In some countries, clubs may also carry out police checks.

- What checks are made? e.g. In England, CRB (Criminal Records Bureau).

- What qualifications do the coaches have? Ideally every team should have at least one qualified FA coach.

- Does the club have a code of conduct? There should be one in place (see Appendix 3).

- Is there an anti-bullying policy? There should be.

- What are the first aid procedures? Every team should have a qualified first aider and an appropriate first aid kit.

- How safe and appropriate is the club's equipment? The under 8s should be using size 3 balls and size 4 balls should be used up to under 14s. Goals should be checked and secured. Do they follow goalpost safety guidelines? (see Appendix 4).

- Does the club hold parent nights? This is a good opportunity to meet and discuss relevant issues.

- What insurance is in place? As a minimum the club should have public liability insurance.

- What are the selection procedures? Does everyone play or is it the same 11 until someone loses form? Is a missed training session a reason to be left out of the team?

Many clubs will provide the above information as part of an induction but if they don't then you need to ask them some/all of the questions on pages 35–6.

▓ Use the list above to compile a checklist that can be used when first visiting your chosen club.

Communicating with the club

Quote │ 'Effective communication must always be two way.'

You now have information on the club/football camp but it is just as important for you to ensure that you provide the club with appropriate information. The types of information you will need to provide are as follows:

- **A club will ask you to complete a membership/registration form. This should include contact details. It is very important to remember to inform the club if these details change.**

- **You will be asked to complete a medical form. This will include any allergies and may also ask for permission to sign on your behalf if treatment to your child is required. Again, if for any reason this information changes, ensure that you inform the club.**

- **Holidays – it will be of help to the club if you can tell the coach as early as possible when you're planning to be away.**

▓ Think about what information your child's coach should know about your child, and write a list of all that you can think of. Come back to the list the following day – often you will have missed a piece of information that will be of use to the coach.

Getting the right philosophy

Every club or football programme should have a philosophy that underpins the programme direction and attitude to the game. As parents and players it is important that we also have a philosophy ourselves and it is vital to find a club that shares this philosophy and the same beliefs.

Some clubs have a win at all costs philosophy even in youth football. This may not suit your child and their particular needs, so consider this aspect carefully. You may prefer a greater emphasis on fun and a philosophy that encourages everyone to play their part.

Many disputes between parents and clubs come when there is a misunderstanding regarding the philosophy and outlook, so make sure that you understand both your own and the club's philosophy.

Quote	'Remember to get the right philosophy to meet the needs of your child.'

In England The FA has a club recognition programme – Charter Standard clubs. To receive The FA Charter Standard kitemark, clubs must demonstrate safe quality practice. This includes:

- **Qualified coaches,**
- **Child protection trained staff and policy,**
- **Codes of conduct,**
- **Fair play.**

There is also a Charter Standard for holiday courses and football camps. When looking for a club/programme in England look out for the Charter Standard. For more information visit **www.TheFA.com/**charterstandard.

Summary

- Decide with your child what sort of club/soccer camp you're looking for.

- Do your research – ask around, visit the website.

- Observe the club in action.

- Don't be afraid to ask questions.

- Get the right philosophy for your child.

Self testers

1 List how, and where, parents can find out information on clubs and programmes.

2 Where can you find information on The FA Charter Standard Programme?

3 What is the recommended coach-to-player ratio?

Action plan

Work out your own philosophy based on the suggestions in this chapter. Discuss it with your child to ensure that you both want the same things from a club or football programme.

Chapter 4

Being involved in the club

THIS CHAPTER WILL:

- Look at how you can get involved in your child's club.
- Consider the importance of the little jobs that you might be able to do.
- Examine how you can become a qualified coach.
- Suggest how you can best use your expertise to help the club.

Quote | 'Without volunteers, football wouldn't exist.'

Ask the majority of volunteers in grassroots football how they became involved with the game and they are all likely to tell a similar story of becoming involved as a way of supporting their child.

Getting involved

There is not a club in the world that wouldn't welcome a new volunteer with open arms. As we will discuss later in this chapter, volunteering doesn't have to mean a 30-year commitment of ten hours a week. No matter how little time you have available, the club will be grateful.

If you do choose to get involved with the club, follow the golden rules:

- Don't overcommit and do what you say you will do.
- Don't use your involvement in the club as an excuse to interfere with the coach and team selection.
- Don't think that because you're a volunteer this guarantees your child's place in the team.
- Be reliable and realistic as to what you are able to do.
- Ask for help if you need it.
- Keep things in perspective, volunteering should be fun!

Don't forget the little jobs

It may be that you have neither the skills nor the time to volunteer for one of the big club jobs such as chairperson or treasurer (see pages 47–52), but even if you only have an hour a week or an hour a month to spare you can still help out and in doing so support the running of the club.

Statistic

Did you know that the conservative estimated value of the volunteer workforce in grassroots football in England is **£500 million** each season?

Here are some ideas of how you can still help out even if you have a limited amount of time to spare:

- Collect the subs for the manager.
- Help with transport, to and from games.
- Assist the coaches with supervision at training or at games.
- Run the line (act as assistant referee).
- Wash the kit (even once a season).
- Help with team administration, such as recording attendances.
- Sell raffle tickets.
- Support fund raising events.
- Organize a one-off fund raiser/special team event.
- Put the nets up before a game and take them down afterwards.
- Sweep the dressing rooms.

Be proactive – take a look at the types of tasks that you may want to assist with and contact the club and volunteer to help.

Becoming a coach

Some of you may have a desire to get involved in the coaching at the club. If you do, talk with the coaches and club secretary to discuss your interest and how you can take it further. One of the first things you will need to do is to go on an FA coaching course. Outside of England the organizations responsible for coaching may differ so you will need to research this, but whatever country you are in, a good starting point will be the current coaching staff at your child's club.

▨   Find out who runs coaching courses in your country. If you're in England visit The FA Learning website at **www.TheFA.com**/FALearning.

We appreciate that throughout the world the process and structure of coaching qualifications will be different. However, in an attempt to provide a useful guide to all readers, we have detailed the qualifications available in England.

Level 1 (club coach)

On this course, you will be supported by an FA coach educator, who will introduce you to the following areas:

- **FA football parents,**
- **Running a club – football administration,**
- **Player and coach development,**
- **Laws of the game,**
- **FA child protection and Best Practice,**
- **FA emergency aid.**

The coach will also introduce you to 23 football games, all with progressions in game and skill. As well as the tuition, you will also receive a coaching video, two books and a CD-ROM.

At the end of the course, you will be asked to run a coaching session during which an experienced coach will observe you and provide you with feedback and advice.

At the end of the course, students are expected to organize sessions that have the following outcomes:

- Safe,
- Fun (with a purpose),
- Organized,
- Appropriate,
- Progressive.

Once you have completed this course and undertaken an assessment, you can then put the skills and ideas you have developed into action at your club.

Best Practice If you're going to be responsible for the development of young players, we would always recommend that you start your coaching career by taking The FA's Level 1 coaching award. Although many parents/coaches have a good understanding of the game the course looks at much more than just training drills and tactics and is a valuable exercise for anyone looking to play a role in coaching. To teach others you need to be in an informed position to start with and this is the best way to start when becoming involved in coaching.

If the 'coaching bug' takes hold, there are lots of other coaching courses you can move onto. For more information visit **www.TheFA.com/** FALearning or see Appendix 2.

Using your expertise

This can be your starting point for getting involved as a volunteer and putting the skills you already have to use at your child's club.

Here are some examples, depending on your profession:

- **Accountant** – You could help with the club's accounts either as treasurer or auditor.

- **Painter/Decorator** – Name a clubhouse that doesn't need a lick of paint!

- **Journalist** – You could help with a press release or with contacts.

- **Business** – Help with writing development/marketing/ business plans and grant applications.

- **Administration** – Help with keeping the club's administration up to date.

- **Computers/IT** – Design posters, develop a club website.

Quote | 'I can't think of any local grassroots club that would ever turn down the opportunity for more volunteers.'

Whatever your job, experience, interests or qualifications, there will be a time when they will be of benefit to the club. However, if the coach or the other volunteers are not aware of your skills then they will be unlikely to ask for your help. If you want to lend a hand and get involved then be proactive and communicate with the other volunteers about what you're good at, so that when the job comes up that suits your skills they will know who to ask.

The big jobs

At some time in your career as a football parent, you may find yourself volunteering for one of the 'big jobs' at the club.

- Club chairperson,
- Club secretary,
- Treasurer,
- Fund raising secretary.

Club chairperson

Who will I be responsible to?

The main committee.

Who will I be responsible for?

Nobody.

What is the role of the club chairperson?

To chair the committee meetings and the Annual General Meeting (AGM). The chairperson should assist the secretary in producing the agendas and head the committee in making decisions for the benefit of the whole club including disciplinary matters.

What else can you tell me about the job?

As the chair of the club, it is essential that you are a strong objective leader. As the supporting officer to the secretary, it is useful for you to have access to a telephone. You may wish to attend a specific training course on how to chair/run meetings.

How much time will I need to give to the job?

Two to three hours per month for meetings.

What sort of tasks are involved?

* Chair committee meetings/AGM.
* Agree the monthly agenda for committee meetings and the AGM.

Club secretary

Who will I be responsible to?

The main committee, through the chairperson.

Who will I be responsible for?

The assistant secretary.

What is the role of the club secretary?

The main purpose of this job is that of principal administrator for the club. The club secretary carries out or delegates all the administrative duties that enable the club and its members to function effectively. The club secretary is a pivotal role within the club, with close involvement in the general running of the club. The secretary and any assistants provide the main points of contact for people within and outside the club on just about every aspect of the club's activities.

What else can you tell me about the job?

As the first point of contact for the club it is helpful for the secretary to be available to take phone calls during the working day. This is a demanding high-profile job that has a major impact on the efficient and effective management of the club. The secretary has contact with a wide range of people from within and outside the club. Representation of the club at outside meetings provides the opportunity to find out what's going on at league and county level. The role of club secretary could be a platform for future volunteering opportunities.

How much time will I need to give to the job?

Approximately eight hours each week and many of these will be at weekends and in the evenings.

What sort of tasks are involved?

- Attending league meetings.
- Affiliating the club to the County FA.
- Affiliating the club to the league(s).
- Registering players to the league(s).
- Dealing with correspondence.
- Organizing and booking match facilities for the season.
- Organizing the club AGM and other club meetings.

- Representing the club at outside meetings, ensuring your clubs' opinions are heard.

Treasurer

Who will I be responsible to?

The main committee.

Who will I be responsible for?

The match/training fees collector.

What is the role of the treasurer?

The main purpose of this job is to look after the finances of the club and regularly report back to members.

What else can you tell me about the job?

The treasurer must be well organized, able to keep records, careful when handling money and cheques, scrupulously honest, able to answer questions in meetings and confident with handling figures. Training courses are often available on a variety of subjects and will be managed through County FAs or relevant local associations.

How much time will I need to give to the job?

Approximately two to three hours per week.

What sort of tasks are involved?

- Collecting subscriptions and all money due to the organization.
- Paying the bills and recording information.
- Keeping up-to-date records of all financial transactions.
- Ensuring that all cash and cheques are promptly deposited in the bank or building society.
- Ensuring that funds are spent properly.
- Issuing receipts for all money received and recording this information.

- Reporting regularly to the committee on the financial position of the club.

- Preparing a year end statement of accounts to present to the auditors.

- Arranging for the statement of accounts to be audited.

- Presenting an end-of-year financial report to the AGM.

- Financial planning including producing an annual budget and monitoring it throughout the year.

- Helping to prepare and submit any statutory documents that are required.

Even if these duties are delegated to a professional officer, the treasurer is still ultimately responsible for the financial aspects of the club. It is up to the treasurer to make sure that any delegated work is done properly.

Fund raising secretary

Who will I be responsible to?

The main committee.

Who will I be responsible for?

The fund raising committee or main committee.

What is the role of the fund raising secretary?

To work with the media secretary (if there is one) to raise awareness of the club in the local area, with the aim of increasing the amount of sponsorship (and therefore funding) that the club receives.

What else can you tell me about the job?

As the fund raising officer it is essential to have good organizational skills. The fund raising officer should be innovative, enthusiastic and be prepared to make a regular time commitment. Prior grant application experience would be useful. Training courses are often available on a variety of subjects and will be managed through County FAs or relevant local associations.

How much time will I need to give to the job?

On average three to four hours each week, but this could rise to eight hours around the time of fund raising events.

What sort of tasks are involved?

- Applying for grants/sponsorships or other forms of financial assistance from organizations such as the Sport England/Football Foundation, local authorities (in England) or commercial companies.

- Co-ordination of fund raising events, if possible two major events per year.

- Ensuring events and activities are properly licensed with local authorities and customs and excise.

- Promotion of fund raising activities in the press (where there is no PR officer).

- Ensuring that funds are properly accounted for and information is passed on to the treasurer.

- The sale of lottery-style draws or raffles on a regular basis, probably weekly.

■ Look at the various roles above and their responsibilities and decide if you could help your child's club in a similar capacity.

LEARNING

Summary

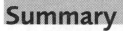

- Remember that clubs always need volunteers.

- No matter how little time you can give, it will be appreciated.

- Don't forget the little jobs you could help with at training or a game.

- If you want to get involved in coaching, find out more information and go on a course.

- Put your skills/experience to good use by helping the club.

- There are a wide variety of courses and people willing to help you if you need it.

- Most importantly being a volunteer can be fun, just ask the millions that do it!

Self testers

1 What are the golden rules you should follow if you get involved in becoming a volunteer for your child's club?

2 Who are the best people to ask if you are interested in coaching?

3 At the end of The FA Level 1 (Club Coach) course, what are the five outcomes for your sessions?

Action plan

Think of your skills and attributes that you could use to help your child's club. Which of the 'little jobs' could you do and would you be prepared to take on?

Chapter 5

Supporting your child

THIS CHAPTER WILL:
- Look at what supporting your child doesn't mean!
- Consider how you can best support your child.
- Make you aware of the resources and equipment needed.
- Help you discover how children learn, and how you can support this.

What supporting your child *doesn't* mean

Whether you're watching your children from the sidelines during a crucial cup semi-final, driving them to training or talking to them at home about the game, your influence as a parent is critical. Too often overenthusiastic parents can let their emotions about the game and their children influence how they communicate and what they say to their child, the coach and the referee.

Quote | 'Football is a sport that is all about passion and competitiveness but that is no excuse for the behaviour of some parents at matches.'

To be a good football parent there are certain rules you should be aware of and should try to follow. Listed below are what we, at The FA, consider to be the golden rules of what not to do:

- **Never showing any encouragement.**
- **Never turning up to watch a match or training.**
- **At games spending the whole game:**
  - **Shouting 'get stuck in' to your child,**
  - **Shouting at the opposition,**
  - **Shouting at your team that they're useless (except for your child!),**
  - **Shouting that your child is useless,**
  - **Shouting that the referee is useless,**

- Shouting that the opposition's manager is useless,
- Shouting that your coach is useless.

■ Be honest and think back to the last time you watched your child play. Did you break any of the golden rules?

Finally, a personal one, particularly for the mums – don't (as mine used to):

- **If your child is injured, run onto the pitch to shout at the player responsible for picking on your child.**
- **At the final whistle give your child a big cuddle and a sloppy kiss. It wouldn't have been so bad, but I was 26 at the time!**

Statistic

In a survey of 9–13 year olds, **54%** felt there was too much pressure to win, **42%** said coaches placed too much pressure on them, **36%** said parents lessened the fun of the game.

What does 'supporting your child' mean?

To put it simply, it is about helping your child to develop through football. Anyone involved in the game knows that football can bring huge benefits to the players, coaches and volunteers, such as a sense of belonging, teamwork, achievement and fitness.

Best Practice To give your child the best chance to enjoy these benefits encourage them to 'be a part of the game' and use your influence to support their needs so that they can continue to develop through football.

Here are some examples of what you can do to support your child:

- Encourage, but don't force your child to take part.
- Understand what your child wants from football, and support this.
- Emphasize the enjoyment and fun of playing the game.
- Praise and reinforce effort and improvement.
- Be a constructive, positive and honest critic.
- Encourage your child to review their performance, and discuss ways for improvement.
- Keep winning in perspective.
- Encourage fair play.

Look at the list above and think about how many of the positive aspects of supporting your child you regularly do.

Resources and equipment

You will need to find a pair of boots for your child that is comfortable and fits well. And whilst the pressure might be to buy the latest model that costs a small fortune, don't over-stretch your budget as there are lots of good products to suit all budgets.

Quote | 'David Beckham doesn't score great free kicks because of his boots but because of his ability and dedication to the sport. You may want to remind your child of this the next time they need a new pair of boots!'

Here are some lists of essential kit that your child will need:

Personal kit

• Appropriate sized football,

• Boots – remember it's what's practical and comfortable, not just fashionable,

- Trainers (particularly for training indoors),
- Tie ups (for the socks),
- Water bottle,
- Shin guards,
- Towel – even if they don't shower as they may still need to dry off, especially if it has been raining.

Additional kit for training

- Shirt,
- Shorts,
- Socks.

Additional kit for a match

- Most clubs provide playing kit,
- Take a tracksuit (again many clubs provide these),
- Rain jacket/warm coat in case your child is a substitute.

Children are not always reliable in their ability to relay messages from the coach or club so make sure that you contact the club to ask what your child's equipment needs will be for the coming season.

Best Practice I am sure that many parents are not always given the correct instructions by their children over issues such as equipment needs, training times or meeting places for away games. To avoid these issues arising look to form regular communication with the coach. This can either be through regular club meetings or by talking before and after matches.

How children learn and how you can support this

We now recognize that children learn in a variety of ways, and this principle is as true in football as in any other activity.

Some people learn best through visual stimulation (video/TV), whilst for others it is through auditory learning (listening) or perhaps they are kinetic/tactile (through feel and touch) learners (practical). However, for most people, learning is the mix of all three.

Quote	'Children learn best through play and by having fun. When planning any training sessions coaches should remember that it must be varied, stimulating and most of all fun!'

Children learn best when the learning features:

- **Student involvement,**
- **Active involvement,**
- **Ownership – they feel it's for them, they are allowed to contribute,**
- **Structure and organization,**
- **It relates to reality – they can see its relevance.**

   Look at the types of practices and training that your child currently participates in and think about how many of the key learning features listed above are covered.

Children tend to be less responsive when the learning environment is:

- **Not planned,**
- **Involves humiliation/sarcasm,**

- The teacher teaches the topic and not the child. This is when, in coaching, you introduce a new progression to the practice but the group still needs to work on the original drill.

Quote | 'Keep training sessions interesting, varied and focused around games in order to keep players engaged.'

As parents, it is important that we encourage our children to experience a variety of learning opportunities. Remembering that we learn through visual stimulation, auditory learning and kinetically (VAK), I have designed a 'Circle of learning', which encourages the player to learn and develop through a variety of mediums as shown on the opposite page.

Remember that children are often easily led, anxious to please and prone to overenthusiasm, and so plenty of praise and positive reinforcement is needed, especially with beginners.

Children often find it hard to understand negative instructions and easier to understand positive reinforcement. This can frequently mean playing

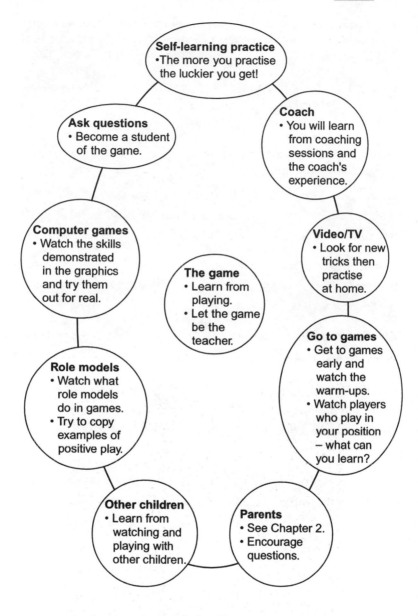

Self-learning practice
•The more you practise the luckier you get!

Ask questions
• Become a student of the game.

Coach
• You will learn from coaching sessions and the coach's experience.

Computer games
• Watch the skills demonstrated in the graphics and try them out for real.

The game
• Learn from playing.
• Let the game be the teacher.

Video/TV
• Look for new tricks then practise at home.

Role models
• Watch what role models do in games.
• Try to copy examples of positive play.

Go to games
• Get to games early and watch the warm-ups.
• Watch players who play in your position – what can you learn?

Other children
• Learn from watching and playing with other children.

Parents
• See Chapter 2.
• Encourage questions.

The circle of learning

down the result and playing up the performance. This reduces the child's anxiety and decreases any worry about failing. Remember that children do not mean to make mistakes; we should accept mistakes as a necessary part of learning.

Burton Haimes, Chairman of AYSO, told me the story of his six-year-old son who, at the end of the game, ran up to him and said 'Daddy, the coach says we won,' then added innocently, 'Daddy, what does that mean?'.

Make sure the players play by the law (the rules); the majority of children as they are introduced to the game will not knowingly infringe the laws of the game. Finally, work with other adults, not against them, and by so doing reinforce positive attitudes among the children.

Summary

- **Be positive.**

- **Don't embarrass your child.**

- **Turn up.**

- **Make sure that your child looks after his/her equipment.**

- **Recognize the different ways your child learns.**

- **Encourage your child to experience the 'circle of learning'.**

Self testers

1 What personal equipment will you need to provide for your child?

2 What are the golden rules that you should never do?

3 What types of learning features engage children to learn more effectively?

Action plan

Assess your child and the ways they learn. What type of a learner are they: visual, auditory, kinetic/tactile learners, or a mixture of the three? Knowing this, what activities are best suited to help them learn and develop?

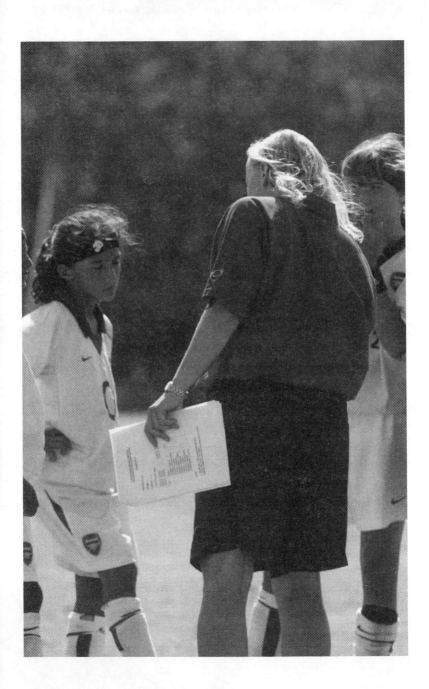

Chapter 6

What children can expect from football parents

THIS CHAPTER WILL:
- Explain why parents are important to football.
- Describe how you can give children a good start from home.
- Show how you can work with the coach to benefit your child's football experience.
- Explain how to make competition better and more appropriate to your child's needs.
- Give advice on supporting the child who shows potential.
- Recommend a parents' code of conduct.

Why parents are important to football

■   Before you read this chapter, try to think of three general ways in which you can have a positive influence on your child, now think of three in a football context.

The parental influence is extremely important and most parents will be aware that they can have both a positive and negative influence dependent on what they do and what they say. One of the most important roles a parent plays in football is helping to shape their child's interest and attitude to the game.

Remember it is important that in developing your child's interest in the game the child is central and the emphasis on winning is secondary. As parents we should be encouraging performance rather than winning and should keep competition in perspective.

If everyone played football solely to win then it wouldn't be long before all but a very few talented players gave up the sport. Even at grassroots level only one team in a league of perhaps 20 will be able to win the championship. Therefore, if winning is your child's primary reason for playing football then there is a high probability that he/she will be disappointed on a regular basis.

Best Practice Ensure that from an early age your child places importance on taking part and having fun rather than on winning. This can be done before your child begins to play sports by putting it into practice as soon as he/she begins to play any kind of game when they are very young.

What can be achieved though as a football parent is improving your child's personal ability and understanding of how to become part of a team and work together to improve both personal and collective performance.

The next time your child plays and loses a game take time to discuss the match without focusing on the result and by discussing what was enjoyed, areas of the game that have improved, what has been learned from the match and how this can be used to develop and improve.

Think about your own philosophy of the game. Which of the following questions would you ask your child following a game and which would you be less likely to ask?

- **Did you win?**
- **Did you enjoy the game?**
- **Did you score?**
- **What was the best part of the game?**
- **Did you play well?**
- **How did you play, what was good, what did you learn?**
- **Who played well?**

Do you place too much emphasis on the winning of a game? You might do this without realizing, but think about how this affects your child's views of the game, especially if all you ask is 'did you win?'

Quote | 'Don't ever just play the game to win. If you do then what happens if you lose?'

Giving children a good start

A supporting and positive home environment provides an excellent launch pad for a child's involvement and enjoyment of the game. Many of the suggestions provided below can be used to support your child in all of his/her interests and hobbies (even in academic studies). Most parents will recognize the suggestions as key aspects of communicating with your child, but they are easy rules to forget. This is especially true if you consider that all most parents want is for their child to be successful and enjoy every aspect of their life.

■ Think about your own experiences at home when you were young. What positive aspects of home life did you benefit from?

Our recommended starting 11 is shown on the opposite page.

How to work with the coach

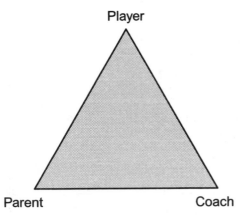

The triangular relationship between player, parent and coach is very simple, but very important at the same time. It is therefore vital that communication is a priority. Good communication is essential between

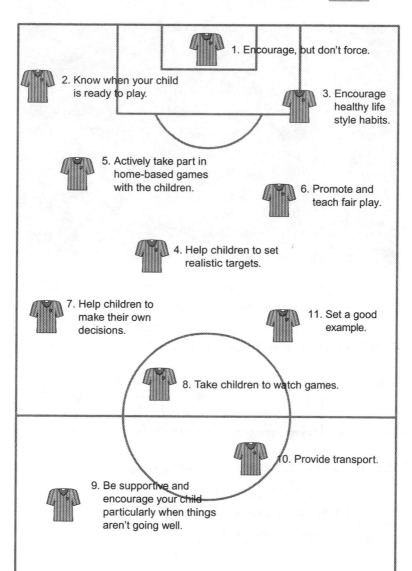

1. Encourage, but don't force.

2. Know when your child is ready to play.

3. Encourage healthy life style habits.

5. Actively take part in home-based games with the children.

6. Promote and teach fair play.

4. Help children to set realistic targets.

7. Help children to make their own decisions.

11. Set a good example.

8. Take children to watch games.

10. Provide transport.

9. Be supportive and encourage your child particularly when things aren't going well.

all points of the triangle in order to give your child the best possible chance of development and to ensure everyone knows what is happening in terms of your child, their development, their performance and any other aspects that might affect them.

Quote	'If in doubt, talk to the coach and other people in your child's club if you have any problems that might affect your child and him/her playing football.'

Here are some golden rules for a better working relationship with the coach:

- Communicate any concerns to the coach.
- Help the coach when asked.
- Refrain from contacting the coach outside of club activities, unless necessary.
- Respect that the coach has a private life.
- Ensure that you have completed a medical consent form.
- Inform the coach about any illness, injury, holidays, change in circumstances etc.

- Make an effort to watch games.
- Make sure your child has the appropriate equipment/clothing.
- Show appreciation for a job well done.

How to make competition better and more appropriate to your child's needs

Essentially football is a competitive game, whether it's in the garden, the playground, the local league or a national cup final. But it is important as football parents that we put competition into perspective for the sake of our children and for ourselves!

There is nothing wrong with healthy competition, the problems occur when the competitive aspect, particularly in children's football, is more important than the game itself. In children's football, competition is a tool to develop participation and performance, it should not be a measure of success (that will develop later) and we should be looking to develop a lifelong interest not a win-at-all-costs environment.

Unfortunately, I have observed too many instances in children's football where the fun, enjoyment and the encouragement to develop good and fair play has been destroyed because of the attitude and behaviour of parents trying to live their lives through their children and their success.

In every park and recreational ground up and down the country the sidelines of the pitch are littered with parents shouting and screaming at the players, referees and coaches. There have been lots of examples of parents fighting amongst themselves and with officials from both the opposing club and their own club.

Football is a game that is passionate and competitive but these should not be ready excuses for emotive parents who set the wrong example every time they watch their children play. Parents should be encouraged to support and encourage their children.

▨ The next time you watch your child play take some time to observe the actions of other parents.

Recently I overheard parents discussing a game their children's team had lost a month previously when the children had probably moved on within the hour and were already looking forward to the next training session and match.

Supporting the child who shows potential

In some cases, children learning the game will develop and improve at a faster rate than their peers. If this is the case and your child looks like he or she is showing potential then we suggest you follow the advice below:

How do you know if your child has potential?

You might observe your child's potential for yourself in training and in games, and your coach may pass comment. In most cases it will be quite obvious to the players and coaching staff at the club if your child has a lot of natural ability for the game. Most professional clubs have a talent identification programme, which recruits players into either their Academy or Centre of Excellence and if your child is good enough this will be the next stage of his or her development.

You may be approached by a club scout, inviting your child to attend a trial, which in turn may lead to an invitation to attend a Development Centre or the Academy (Centre of Excellence). Alternatively your coach may be able to make contact with a professional club on the player's behalf and invite the club to watch the player. If this happens you must consider the following:

1 **Make sure that both the club and the school are kept informed if you are approached by a professional club.**
2 **Your child has achieved a great deal in getting this far but remember that the club will be looking at hundreds of players in a season. Therefore, just because your child has a trial, it is no guarantee that he/she will be selected.**

An Academy director at a professional club once told me that he tells his newly recruited players, 'Today you're the best. Tomorrow my job is to find someone better.' At this level of the game, football is very competitive and for the thousands of young players registered with Centres of Excellence only a handful will ever make it to the top of their profession.

From grassroots player to international star

Below is a diagram of the girls' player pathway, which shows the steps at each level and how at each step as the standard increases the number of girls playing becomes fewer.

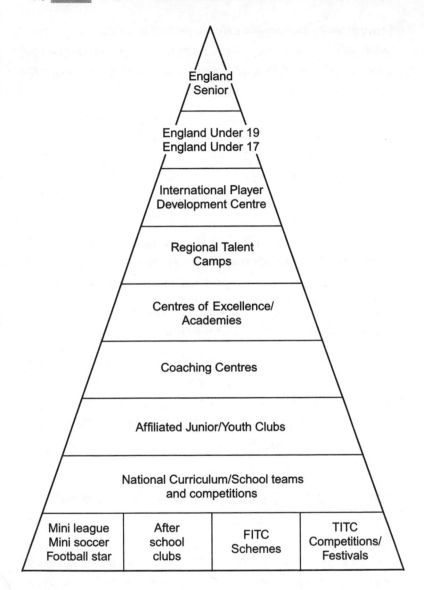

Control your own ambitions

It is all too easy for the parents of talented children to become too involved in their own personal ambition for their children rather than considering their children's own ambition. Make sure that you are never too pushy, and remember it is your child's life, not your own. The best thing that you can do is to be supportive and don't get carried away with your own ideas of what your child can or might be able to do. Let your child make his/her own decisions about achievements and aspirations. You should be there to help your child by offering advice and guidance.

| Quote | 'Have you ever asked your child what he/she wants out of playing football and if he/she has a realistic ambition that they are aiming towards?' |

Managing your child's ambitions

The way you manage your child's ambitions is extremely important. We all need to have goals and believe in ourselves, but part of your role is to be realistic. This will depend on your child's age, their rate of development, and the ability already shown. It is difficult to strike the balance that is needed as a parent, because you will always want to encourage and help your child maximize his/her potential, whilst at the same time minimize the risk of your child being disappointed.

It is the role of the football parent to be aware of all the possible outcomes that your child may have to face and to be ready for the tears of either joy or disappointment. For many talented children set-backs will be part of the game and it is often how they react to these that determine how far they will go in achieving their dreams. Football is all about opinions and the game is full of stories of players released by managers at one club to become a superstar years later at another. Players can be released for many reasons and I am sure that if you're the parent of a talented child you may not agree, but if such an event arises don't focus on the negative and make sure that you are there for your child.

Poor coaching

How do you deal with an overenthusiastic coach? Overenthusiasm, shouting at players and highly-emotive actions are not just the character traits of some football parents. Coaches can also be guilty of setting a poor example and if your child's team has such a coach then you should look for ways of communicating your concerns.

You should not be afraid to approach the coach to discuss your worries about his/her actions if you feel that this is having a negative effect on your child's development or enjoyment. If this doesn't work then we suggest you approach a senior club official.

Achieving a balance

How do you help your child maintain a balanced life? If your child is showing great potential then it is likely that they will start to play more often. Training will become more regular, matches more frequent and the demand on your child's time even greater. However, it is your role as a football parent to ensure that there is some balance.

Quote	'A very small percentage of Academy players will become full-time professionals so ensure your child has a 'plan B', just in case.'

Most importantly, ensure that your child keeps up with school work and maintains their friendship groups. You may need to agree a sensibly-structured programme that allows time for all these activities and also gives your child some spare time. In most cases coaches or Academy directors also recognize the needs of the child to have a life away from football and will support the parent's wishes.

■ Together with your child develop a balanced programme, which takes into account training, matches, school demands and other pastimes. Ensure that your child has spare time to relax. If there is insufficient spare time we would suggest discussing with your child the possibility of cutting down on some activities.

Dropping out

What do I do if my child wants to drop out? Well to start with, don't shout and threaten them! Talk to your child and the coach to try to understand the reasons behind the decision and ask your child how he/she came to the decision. There may well be problems that no one was aware of, which may be easy to solve or it may be that the child just wants to have a break and stop playing for a while. It may be appropriate to arrange a meeting with the coach and/or the Academy director so that all parties, including the child, can reach an informed decision. Whatever the outcome of the meeting, as the football parent you must make sure that you give your child your full backing and support.

Best Practice By observing the rules of continuous, honest and open communication between the player, the parent and the coaching staff, it is hoped that such a situation as described on page 79 would not suddenly occur 'out of the blue'. If you think your child is having difficulties then be proactive and spend time with them as problems that are discussed early and shared between parent and player are often much easier to solve.

Parents' code of conduct

It is important that parents set a good example. To help with this we suggest that you follow The FA parents' code of conduct which has been developed to provide parents with positive ideas on supporting their child and football (see below).

As parents we can influence our children's enjoyment and success in football. It is important to remember that however good a child becomes at football, as a parent you should reinforce the message within your child's club that positive encouragement will contribute to:

- **Children enjoying football.**
- **A sense of personal achievement.**
- **Greater self-esteem.**
- **An improvement in the child's skills and techniques.**

A parent's expectations and attitudes have a significant bearing on a child's attitude towards:

- **Other players,**
- **Officials,**
- **Managers,**
- **Spectators.**

Best Practice Ensure that other parents within your child's club are always positive and encouraging towards all of the children and not just their own.

Encourage other parents to:

- Applaud the opposition as well as your own team.
- Avoid coaching their child during the game.
- Not to shout and scream.
- Respect the referee's decision.
- Give attention to each of the children involved in football not just the most talented.
- Encourage everyone to participate in football.

A colleague from America told me that in their organization referees have had cards printed, which are given to parents who argue. The cards say, 'You obviously know a lot about the game. Ever thought of being a voluntary referee?'

Ensure that all of the parents within your club agree and adhere to the club's code of conduct. By all agreeing and sticking to the code of conduct it will help create a positive environment to play and learn the game.

Summary

- **Be positive and give lots of encouragement.**

- **Provide a good start for your child beginning at home.**

- **Work with, not against, the coach, don't interfere and remember to communicate with them. A little help would also be appreciated.**

- **Keep competition healthy and in perspective.**

- **If your child has potential, be supportive and realistic but don't push.**

- **Keep to your code of conduct.**

Self testers

1 List as many golden rules as possible for communicating with the coach.

2 Why is it important to manage your child's ambitions?

3 How should you deal with an overenthusiastic coach?

Action plan

If your club does not already have a code of conduct then arrange a meeting with interested parents and coaching staff at the club to discuss the principle of implementing one.

Chapter 7

LEARNING

What football parents can expect from children

THIS CHAPTER WILL:
- Look at a child's development at different ages.
- Consider how children's development impacts on them as players.
- Help you consider what you can expect from your child depending on age.

'Why can't he head the ball?' I am unable to keep count of the number of times I have overheard this question from parents of young children!

Quote	'Within any group of children there could be a four-year development range. For example, in a group of under 11s, whilst some will display the average, others could still be displaying the characteristics of an under 9, whilst others could be considered an under 13 in terms of development. In time, this will usually equal out, but parents and coaches need to be aware of this.'

In the following pages we have highlighted the particular characteristics of the different age groups involved in youth football. This will give you an idea of what you can expect from your child and how you can use this information to support their development and encourage their continued participation.

Under 8s

Characteristics	What does this mean?
Excitable	Expect lots of energy and running around from your child.
Enthusiastic	Build on this, encourage the players, don't be negative, and focus on development and participation and don't be driven by results.
Egocentric	Don't expect lots of passes and teamwork. Encourage your child to concentrate on developing his/her individual skills.
Talkative	Encourage them to ask questions and communicate on the pitch.
Short concentration span	They will get bored quickly, so organize lots of fun yet purposeful games.
Limited understanding of space	Expect everyone to chase the ball.
Sensitive to criticism	Be aware of this sensibility.
Lack of decision-making ability	The more decisions you give them, the less likely they will be to make one. Four vs. four or three against three is best at this age group.
Difficulty in judging the speed of moving objects	Expect them to air kick and miss the ball. Make sure you don't criticize them if they do this, but suggest ways to help them to avoid doing this.
Undeveloped strength	Don't expect many 20 m cross-field passes and work on short passing and shooting.

Quote | 'I wish I had a pound for every time I've heard a coach spend the entire training session telling the players to be quiet, and the entire game complaining that the players won't talk to each other.'

Statistic

The average adult can concentrate for 20 minutes, so don't expect a seven year old to concentrate for more than ten minutes.

Best Practice Give your child the choice between a theme park, a day at the zoo, the circus, or a trip to the seaside. You will still be there two hours later before a decision is made. Give a choice of two and you will get an answer! Young children have not fully developed their decision-making skills so be aware of this. Don't get frustrated if they find it hard to make decisions. Make it easier for young children by giving them limited choices.

Under 10s

Characteristics	What does this mean?
Golden age of learning	Encourage questions and set challenges to test and stretch the player.
Increased awareness of others	Increase decision-making options and understanding of what children can do to progress play. Move to six against six or seven against seven and expect more passes.
Enthusiastic	Don't stifle your child, instead use this enthusiasm to encourage and develop ability. It might also be a good idea to develop this enthusiasm by going to watch other matches to get a different experience of the game.
More attentive	You can go into more in depth in coaching sessions as the child will have a longer concentration span and will absorb more information. But make sure you explain and check his/her understanding.
Enjoyment of challenges	Stretch children both physically and mentally by using more advanced coaching games.
Increased strength	Expect more long passes.
Loss of flexibility	It is important to recognize that this happens and therefore be as vigilant as ever in remembering the warm-up!

Under 14s

Characteristics	What does this mean?
Able to develop team play	Develop positional play.
Enjoy problem solving	Don't provide the answers – in training set a problem, and encourage them to solve this. We need to encourage problem solving in players as we need them to thrive and adapt in a game when we can't be on the pitch with them!
Peer pressure	Be aware of the growing influence of a child's peers.
Identify others' strengths and weaknesses	This can be both positive and negative. It will be a challenge as to how you encourage the player to evaluate performance in a positive way. This lies in the ability to recognize the concepts of team play.
Competitive	The players want to participate in and enjoy competition and the physical challenge that comes

Characteristics	What does this mean?
Competitive (*continued*)	with this but remember to keep competition in perspective. It's nice to win, but not at any cost! There are lessons to be learned from defeat – turn it into a positive learning experience.
Physical change	Be aware and sensitive to the impact puberty may have on the individual. At this age there could be a large difference in size and strength between players – this will usually equal out in time. As a child has a growth spurt, he/she may become weaker – keep an eye on this. Children of this age could also be susceptible to injury as the muscle and bone develop at different rates.

Over 15s

Characteristics	What does this mean?
Growing stronger	Players are reaching adulthood and have fewer growth spurts.
Greater mental strength	Players will have a greater ability to cope with tough game situations.
The need for physical challenge	As the body becomes stronger so does the ability to meet physical challenge. Part of this is to test yourself against others.
More tactically aware	Players will, by this stage, have settled on a preferred position. They will be more aware of their role in the team and of how this supports the roles of those around them.
More analytical	Players are able to review their own performance and the performances of others, including that of the coach. This can be challenging, but should be encouraged.

Characteristics	What does this mean?
More competitive	This links into the need for physical challenge. Players in this age group want to compete and beat themselves.
Changes in personal life	During this period young people will be facing lots of changes in their life, such as moving from school to college or work. This may lead to new friendship groups. Often in these circumstances the football club can be the one constant in their life.

Best Practice Remember that for all age groups, we must support players to develop, improve and encourage them to think for themselves.

▨ Table 2 shows a number of football techniques/skills. Take the time to watch some children's games at different age groups. Observe the skills you see in different age groups and complete the grid accordingly by placing a tick everytime you see the skill performed.

Table 2

SKILL	AGE GROUP								
	Under 8			Under 10			Under 14		
	Sometimes	Often	Always	Sometimes	Often	Always	Sometimes	Often	Always
Short pass									
Long pass									
Lifted pass									
Dribble									
Running with the ball									
Change of direction									
Shot									
Tackle									
Goalkeeper catch									
Diving to save									
Heading									
Timing a pass									
Intercepting									

This exercise should help you to know what you might expect from your child as they reach each age group.

Tables 3–6 show how a child's age and development can impact on his/her footballing skills.

Table 3 **Passing**

Age	How is it performed?	Common mistakes	Implications for the coach
6–7 year olds	• Not frequently • Lots of chasing • Lots of touches of the ball	• Not passing, it's running with the ball • Pass almost by accident • Predominantly only use one foot	Encourage the players to pass in small games.
10–11 year olds	• More passes • Creating space • Two to three touches then a pass	• Use wrong part of foot • Don't always look • Still one-footed • Not always active	Look to improve techniques within the games.

Table 4 **Shooting**

Age	How is it performed?	Common mistakes	Implications for the coach
6–7 year olds	• Not frequently • Lots of touches • Get as near as possible to the goal	• Try to run the ball into the goal	• Set up games which encourage lots of shots. • Maybe in this game set out an area, say 8 yards out and they must shoot outside of this area.

Age	How is it performed?	Common mistakes	Implications for the coach
10–11 year olds	• Will be more willing to try and shoot • Less touches before a shot • Willing to try from a greater distance	• Using preference foot • Using only one part of the foot	• Set up games with lots of shooting situations. • Add conditions of two touch then shoot. • Encourage the use of both feet. • Encourage players to strike the ball with the 'laces' part of the foot.

Table 5 **Tackling**

Age	How is it performed?	Common mistakes	Implications for the coach
6–7 year olds	• By accident • Everyone chasing the ball and they get in the way!	• Can tackle own player! • Can be threatening	• Use games that encourage people to win the ball back. • Make it fun.
10–11 year olds	• Starting to recognize and understand tackling	• Dive in/go to ground	• Encourage player to be patient, keep standing and wait for opportunity to steal the ball. • Be on the look out for counter attack.

Table 6 **Heading**

Age	How is it performed?	Common mistakes	Implications for the coach
6–7 year olds	• Not very often • Usually by accident!	• Eyes closed • Let the ball hit them	• Introduce heading gently – use a balloon or beach ball. • Start by them heading the ball from their hands.
10–11 year olds	• Start to see more of in the game • Will usually let the ball bounce!	• Don't use forehead • Still, in many cases, letting the ball hit them	• As you see heading happening more in the game, introduce it more in your training. • Use the appropriate size ball. • Person A serves to person B who heads it back. • Encourage the player to use the forehead and keep their eyes open.

Summary

- There can be up to a four-year development range within any age group.

- There are development characteristics in children that will influence their football development.

- Don't expect lots of passing in the under 8s but expect everyone to follow the ball.

- The golden age of learning begins at ten.

- The under 14s will begin to develop team play and enjoy problem solving.

- As a child reaches 15 they are looking for greater challenges.

- Watch games to see what children at different age groups can achieve – this will help you to be realistic about what to expect from your child.

- Encourage your child to adhere and respect the players' code of conduct (see Appendix 3).

Self testers

1   If your child suffers from a short concentration span, what tactics can you employ to ensure that they continue to develop their skills?

2   If your child is becoming very enthusiastic, what is the best way of dealing with this and making the most of their interest?

3   If your child is getting increasingly competitive, what can you
    do to ensure this is controlled and kept in perspective?

Action Plan

Depending on the age of your child, consider the characteristics
listed in this chapter and note which ones they are displaying.
Make a plan of the key things you need to do to either enhance or
control these characteristics.

Chapter 8

The training of young players

THIS CHAPTER WILL:
- Give you an understanding of the concept of trainability.
- Provide information on when to train youngsters and in what aspects of the game.
- Help you to remember that the game is fun!

It must be clearly understood when training young players that they are not 'mini-adults'. This can easily be forgotten.

As children grow and mature, their physical needs and capabilities change. Boys and girls differ in their responses to exercise which are more apparent following puberty. Strength levels are generally greater in males due to the smaller percentage of body fat while a smaller heart and blood volume contributes to a higher heart rate response to exercise in females. From as young as five or six years of age there are gender-related differences in children's responses to exercise.

These differences are magnified as boys and girls grow and it is vital that anyone involved in their development and training understands how to nurture talent whilst protecting the young players' welfare as they continue to develop physically.

Growth and maturation are closely related, although the two are totally different processes. Growth refers to an increase in the size of the body or its parts; maturation is progress towards the mature or adult biological state. Growth does not stop when maturity is reached but continues throughout life as in nearly every tissue and organ there is a cycle of growth, death and regeneration.

The principles according to which adults train and play cannot be directly applied to young players because of the differences in the maturity of the skeletal, muscular and cardiovascular systems. Training must be adapted to their development; being progressed slowly while laying down suitable foundations. This fact may easily be ignored by parents or well-meaning coaches who coax and cajole their pre-adolescent protégés to swifter, higher and stronger competitive levels.

Growth dynamics to show average annual growth rates in boys

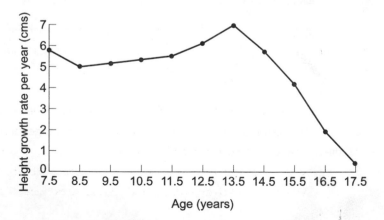

The graph on the previous page highlights that 'growth spurts' occur from ten years through to 15 years of age. However, it should be noted that significant growth occurs from 8.5 years through to 15.5 years of age and continues past 18 years of age for some.

Increased potential for injury

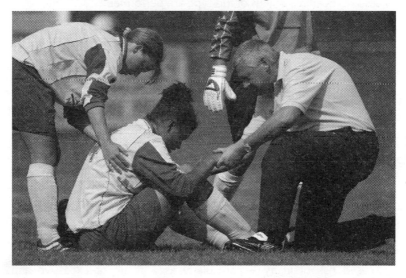

It is during the early and adolescent years of life that the body's muscles and bones develop and grow. The young player may be more susceptible to injury during this period. Bone in young players is still not mature; it has not yet fully ossified and is under considerable stress from strong maturing muscle action.

Injuries resulting from overplay (playing too regularly with little rest) usually affect the parts of the skeleton that constitute attachments of tendons and ligaments. In children and adolescents who participate in regular training and competition, the muscles develop more rapidly than the skeleton. This may be hazardous due to the unusual stress it puts on the skeleton.

Bone grows faster than soft tissues such as muscles and tendons, which become tighter with growth, particularly during 'growth spurts'. This loss of flexibility can be a factor in increasing the risk of injury.

Football involves the forceful actions of running, jumping, landing, kicking and fast direction changes. The chance of injury can increase if excessive repetitive actions of this type are performed.

Because of the stages of development that the body is going through and particularly up until the age of 14/15, you need to be aware of the demands placed on young players and ensure their training methods are adapted to the development of players.

Statistic

Football is now the most popular sport played by girls as well as boys.

Different training needs for young players – keep it varied

As highlighted above, as young players' bodies develop there is an increased risk of injury – particularly as a result of excessive and repetitive movements that focus on a particular part of the body.

For example, if during a 90-minute training session, the coach runs 3×10 minute sessions of jumping and heading practice there would be an increased chance of injury to the knees or ankle joints. This is because this would be the area of the body taking the impact of this particular training drill.

If the same coach had devised a 90-minute training session that only had one jumping and heading practice, one turning with the ball practice and one shooting practice, the chances of injury would be reduced. This is because different areas of the body would be taking the impact of these training drills.

If training sessions are kept varied and interesting it will not only help young players to improve their chance of avoiding injury but should also assist the young players' interest and motivation levels.

The Official FA Guide to Basic Team Coaching title in this series looks at a variety of training sessions suitable for young players and will assist anyone looking to increase variety in their training sessions.

■ If you're involved in the coaching of young players think about how varied you make your training sessions.

The need to understand younger players

The young player is physiologically unique from the adult and must be considered differently. Generally, the youngster will adapt well to the same type of training routine used by the mature athlete, but training programmes for children and adolescents should be designed specifically for each age group, bearing in mind the developmental factors associated with their age.

The graph on page 100 shows growth velocity for stature for boys. Statural growth occurs at a constantly decelerating rate – the child is getting bigger, but at a slower rate. The rate reaches its lowest point just before initiation of the adolescent spurt.

Young players' growth patterns result in variations in anatomical factors such as limb length, the stability of muscle-tendon-bone attachments, relative muscle/bone length and vulnerability to bone at growth plates or muscle attachments. There are also physiological factors such as decreased cardiovascular endurance, muscle strength and flexibility.

Decreased flexibility is common in young players. It is generally caused by the different rates of growth in bones and muscles, so that the muscles are relatively shorter than the bones. The areas subject to the greatest growth are the back and the legs, therefore muscles acting on these areas i.e. the quadriceps, hamstrings, iliotibial band, and back extensor muscles are most likely to show this tightness.

Long-term development of young players

The section below summarizes the three phases of development and the types of training and areas of development that should be focused on in each phase.

Fundamental phase (6–11 years)

The fundamental phase of development is a multilateral phase that lays a foundation on which future development is built. This is the time when the young player will begin to learn the basic skills that will continue to be used throughout his/her playing career.

This is also the stage at which the young player is least developed physically and therefore has limited endurance (stamina) and strength levels, therefore training should be focused on technique and playing rather than fitness and strength training.

Football should be all about having fun, doing something you enjoy and being part of a team and so everyone needs to ensure that players enjoy their first experiences of the game.

The key implications in coaching this age group are summarized below.

- Basic skills should be developed, such as passing, shooting, heading, controlling the ball, turning with the ball etc.
- Activities should be of a short duration with endurance being developed through play and games and not endurance training.
- Use slow progression in hopping and jumping activities and strength training should be limited to technique development.
- Specific activities and games should emphasize co-ordination.

Training to train phase (11–14 years)

During this phase of development, athletic formation begins to take place with the body and its capacities develop rapidly.

This is also the time when the percentage of players that begin to drop out increases as players begin to find other activities; computer games, socializing with friends, other sports and discovery of the opposite sex demand more of their time, so there is a need to ensure that players maintain their interest in the game.

Ensuring training sessions are still fun, varied and involve competitive elements such as five-a-side matches will help maintain interest and hopefully begin to keep more teenagers in the game.

The key implications in coaching this age group are summarized below.

- **Remember that chronological age may not be the most appropriate way to group players as young people develop at different rates so compare height, body mass, strength etc. instead.**

- Players should learn how to train during this phase, including physical, technical, tactical and ancillary capacities (e.g. warm-up, cool-down, nutrition, rest, recovery etc.).

- Some previously learned skills might need refinement, as limb growth will impact on technique, balance and co-ordination.

- Focus on speed work either during or immediately after the warm-up and not when players are tired at the end of a training session.

Training to compete phase (14–20 years)

The biggest changes in training occur during this phase. The exercises undertaken are aimed at development, but with the intensity and volume of work gradually increasing.

The key implications in coaching this age group are summarized below.

- **Aerobic and anaerobic systems become fully developed and can be trained for maximum output.**

- Strength training can be maximized to improve overall strength development and training of the nervous system should be optimized.
- Learning how to compete is important, incorporating all technical, tactical and ancillary components into performance.

As highlighted in the 'Training to train' phase, as the young players' age increases more players drop out of the game and the roles of the coach and parent are critical to maintaining the interest and motivation of the young player.

Football as a sport has many positive outcomes for those that regularly participate, including:

- Fitness,
- Teamwork,
- Competitiveness,
- Responsibility to others (i.e. teammates),
- Social skills.

This is why we need to maintain the interests of young players in this age group at such a crucial time in their development and the coach, parents and teachers are central to this.

Long-term development

In the long-term development programme it should be apparent that there is a gradual change from general to specific conditioning of players as they pass through the various stages of athletic development.

You should be aware that at the younger age groups the players' training should concentrate on the technical aspects of the game as this is when basics skills are learned, while ensuring training is varied and the emphasis is on playing and having fun.

Best Practice Don't expect too much too soon and the long-term development of the player should be the overall objective.

As the players develop physiologically, training can begin to develop the physical aspects required, such as strength and stamina throughout specific and targeted training. However, remember that varied and competitive elements of training will be necessary to maintain the interest and motivation of players.

Early vs. late specialization

The graph below shows the difference between early and late specialization sports. In this example we have used gymnastics to compare with football.

Early specialization explained

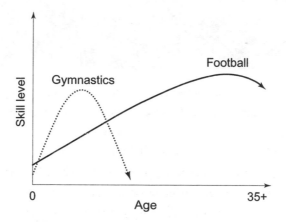

In gymnastics the training of young athletes is more intensive than in football and begins at a much earlier age as most gymnasts will only participate in competitions until their late teens, although many male competitors will continue to their early and mid 20's. When compared to football gymnastics is an early specialization sport.

The potential playing career of a footballer is much longer than a gymnast's, especially at grassroots level with players regularly participating well in to their 40s. Even within the professional game there are many examples of footballers continuing to participate at the highest level long after their 35th birthday. For example, Paulo Maldini, Rob Lee, Paul Ince, Stuart Pearce and Colin Cooper.

In football players improve and mature at different rates and in many cases the player's position (e.g. goalkeeper, defender etc.) has a major impact on the time taken to specialize. For example, many experts would argue that central defenders peak in their late 20s as key attributes other than the purely physical, such as decision-making and composure, take time to develop.

If a player does not develop until his mid to late 20s, you should realize that young players, and especially those just starting to play competitive football, should be able to have fun whilst learning the technical aspects of the game through playing matches and specific technical practices. They should not have to spend large portions of their training time working at the physical aspects until their bodies reach a sufficient maturity.

It should also be remembered that playing regularly will help younger players to develop the physical aspects of their game naturally. Through training matches and competitive play young players will begin to develop stamina, strength and speed while also learning the skills that will improve their enjoyment of the game.

How much sport does your child play?

For many children football may be only one of a number of sports that the child plays on a regular basis. The sports available to children to play in an organized capacity are greater than at any time in the past and this can mean that although a child only plays football a couple of times a week his/her overall sporting schedule may be increasing their chances of overloading type injuries.

Although we, at The FA, always promote a fit and active, healthy lifestyle involving plenty of exercise, it is important that young players allow their bodies time to recover from exercise.

Maintaining a sensible balance of rest and play should ensure that the chances of injury are reduced and that the playing careers of young players are extending into their 20s, 30s and 40s with a reduced number of injuries that are typically associated with over training.

▨ Think about how much sport your child plays and look at whether he/she allows time in their schedules to rest and recover.

▨ If you're involved in coaching, ask the players how many sports they play and how often, in order to gain an insight into the stresses they place on their bodies.

Summary

- Young players are not 'mini-adults'.

- As children grow and mature, their physical needs and capabilities change.

- Training must be tailored and aligned to the development of the young players' physical needs and capabilities.

Self testers

1 Why is there an increased risk of injury for younger players?

2 What are the differences between early and late specialization sports?

3 When should a child be learning the basic skills of football?

Action plan

Make sure you are aware of the training programme for your child and ensure that it meets their developmental needs, their physical capabilities and that it is FUN!

The FA

LEARNING

Chapter 9

Using the experience of the football parent

THIS CHAPTER WILL:
- Look at three case studies written by football parents.
- Examine the football parent's philosophy.
- Consider the values and competences of football parents.

What experiences can help you be a football parent?

Football parents – some real stories

Here are three real stories from volunteers who became involved as football parents and still get hours of fun and enjoyment through their voluntary involvement in the game.

Case study 1

I became a volunteer in girls' football because my daughter could no longer play mixed football. The nearest girls' club was over 15 miles away and she was only ten. Someone told me that the local men's team was looking to start a girls' side so I contacted them and was told that it could start as soon as I arranged the sessions. The club was born in December 1995 with around 15 girls in the car park at Redditch United.

Over the last eight years it has gone from my husband Tim doing the training and me everything else – neither of us being qualified, to having 120 or more girls training with 30 or more coaches and an army of volunteers keeping the club moving forward.

What have I got out of it? A headache from not having enough players each week and then from having so many we have to start a new team what seems like every week. But nothing gives me greater pleasure than seeing all the girls having the opportunity to play the beautiful game. The experience I have gained has enabled me to become a girl's and women's Football Development Officer – so now I even get paid for the job I love. I am sure one day I will have to get a proper job, but until then I'll put up with the headaches.

Julie Leroux

Case Study 2

I got involved with Jersey Wanderers when my son began playing junior football. The club needed volunteer helpers and, as a past player, I wanted to put something back into the local game. On the coaching side, I gain tremendous satisfaction from seeing how youngsters come through our junior ranks and progress into our senior teams. I also believe that football clubs provide a valuable development opportunity for youngsters, not only in improving their soccer skills, but also helping them learn the importance of teamwork, self-motivation and having a positive attitude. This was something I wanted to be part of.

When the Charter Standard programme was launched I recognized that by following these guidelines, and experience from my job, I would be able to assist the club in putting together a business plan and a long-term development strategy. It is with immense satisfaction that I look back at the advances we have made and how we now have a platform for moving forward on a sustainable and progressive basis.

Winning the National Administrator award is fantastic, not only for the personal recognition, but more so that it recognizes the progress that Jersey Wanderers has made by following Charter Standard principles and the work and high standards being set in Jersey by our football development officer, Brian Oliver.

Bob Lawrence
Jersey Wanderers FC

Case Study 3

I have been involved with Easton Girls FC for three years. I became involved through my daughter's interest in football and this season I am jointly managing the under 10s football team. I really enjoy my involvement with the club and being part of its development.

Easton is an ethically and culturally diverse inner-city area and the team reflects this. As well as being a great team game it is good to see how the girls' individual skills develop. I really get a buzz out of watching the girls play.

I love the passion, excitement and the highs and lows the team goes through. I have met other parents, friends and people involved in football clubs and the league.

Football encourages a team spirit in girls, co-ordination, co-operation, confidence, self-esteem and friendship.

Most of all I am involved because it is great fun and for the sense of achievement I get from being part of a local community team.

I really love football.

Kim Graham

▨   Ask your child what sort of football parent they want you to be?

The FA football parent's philosophy

All football parents should share and work towards The FA's vision, values and competences.

Our shared aim in football is to **use the power of football to build a better future.**

As football parents:

- Our **values** should be **responsive** to the needs of our child, all players and football in general.
- We should be confident in our approach and show **courage** in our actions.
- We should be open to new ideas and be able to take on board other views.
- Our philosophy should be **inclusive**, encouraging everyone to enjoy and love this great game.
- Everyone must be **accountable** to those they work with and to football and the community at large.
- We should be **challenging** ourselves to bring out the best in our children. We should be **passionate** for the game and pass on this passion, encouraging others to develop a lifelong love of the game.
- Our shared competences are those of **leadership**, taking **responsibility** and showing direction.
- We should be aware of **change orientation** and using change to help us meet our vision.
- We should be able to **communicate** and **influence** those around us, taking **ownership** of the game. We should also demonstrate that contribution far outways achievement in the game.
- We should be **innovativ**e in our approach as football parents.

Competences and values expected of a football parent

Responsive

- Understand the needs of your children.
- As a 'garden coach' ensure you use appropriate practice.

Achievement

- Knowledge,
- Confidence,
- Capability,
- Independence,
- Understanding,
- Proactive,
- Respectful,
- Focused,
- High standards.

Courage

- Set standards,
- Raise standards,
- Do what's right for the game,
- No fear of failure.

Change orientation

- Be open to new ideas.
- Encourage your child to be open.
- Encourage your child to take responsibility.

Inclusive

- Football is for everyone.

Passionate

- Love of the game,

- Enthusiasm,
- Instil this passion in your children.

Accountable

- Football parents should be accountable to their children, the coaches and to football.

Challenging

- Attitude,
- Ethics,
- Improve oneself,
- Improve others,
- Open minds,
- Use imagination.

Leadership

- Be positive,
- Lead by example,
- Role model,
- Keep everyone involved,
- Encouragement,
- Be a volunteer.

Communication

- Not just verbal,
- Let the game be the teacher,
- Listening skills,
- Appropriate language,
- No jargon.

Ownership

- Take responsibility,
- Set an example,
- Show commitment.

Innovation

- Improvization,
- Problem solving,
- Development,
- Thinking ahead.

Summary

- Being a football parent can be great fun.

- The more you get involved, the more fun you can get out of it – remember the case studies.

- Work to FA competences and values.

- Try to follow the football parent's philosophy.

Self testers

1 What are the six leadership values expected of football parents?
2 Who should football parents be accountable to?
3 As a football parent, how should you communicate?

Action plan

Can you write a case study of your experience as a football parent? How did you get involved? What benefits did it bring and how did you help your child? Write a brief case study.

Chapter 10

Maintaining teenage interest

THIS CHAPTER WILL:
- Explain how to avoid overuse injuries.
- Look at the reasons behind teenagers stopping playing.
- Provide guidance on supporting the move into adult football.

Quote | 'The problem with youth is that it is wasted on the young.'

For those of us who are past 30 and almost 40, we long to play without the aches and pains and we'll try anything to get just a few more years of playing in the over 35s or the over 40s team. In fact, I've often wondered when I'll hear of the first over 60s league!

So for us the surprise is that many teenagers leave this great game, give it up and move on. Although some may return later, for others as they reach 14 and older, that will be it and they will have played their last competitive 11 vs. 11 game.

▨ If you are no longer playing football ask yourself why you stopped playing. Can you list the reasons for your decision?

Overuse injury

One reason that some young people stop playing is because of injury. Of particular concern, especially to the football parent, is the overuse injury.

An overuse injury is an injury involving certain bones or muscles/tendons of the body, which develops over a period of time due to too much repetitive activity. The injury becomes worse with continued activity at the same level and will continue unless correct medical advice and treatment is followed.

Overplay is the term used to describe the cause of such injuries and young players are particularly vulnerable to overuse injuries caused by overplay. It is the responsibility of everyone involved in the development of young players to look after the child's medical interests.

Remember when dealing with children that they are exactly that – children, not small adults – and training and match programmes should reflect this. You can refer to another book in this series, *The Official FA Guide to Fitness for Football*, for more information on fitness and injuries.

Quote | 'Children do not stop growing until they are at least 18, and it is important to remember this especially when you are putting physical demands on them that their bodies may not be able to cope with.'

The risk of injuries caused by overuse is now known to be considerable and such injuries will certainly hinder a young player's development. Regrettably, promising careers may have been prematurely ended due to overuse at an early age. Therefore it is important that as a football parent, you are aware of the potential risks, and make sure your child strikes a balance between playing and resting, so that the chance of overuse injuries are minimized.

The four main causes of overuse injuries have been identified as the following:

- **Load,**
- **Technique,**
- **Posture,**
- **Equipment.**

The young player is vulnerable to injury during periods of growth and maturity. Bone in young players is not yet fully developed and is under stress from strong muscular actions. In children and adolescents who participate in regular training and competition the muscles develop more rapidly than those of the same age that do not train and compete. Loss of flexibility increases the chance of injury by putting further stress on the developing skeleton. The faster growers are particularly at risk.

Factors to consider

- Bone grows faster than muscle and other soft tissue.
- Muscle matures more quickly in young athletes than in non-athletes.
- During growth spurts, as bone grows faster than soft tissue, there is an additional risk to the pre-adolescent who loses flexibility and the pull on the soft bone increases.
- Growth plates – the areas where bone grows – are weakest during puberty and this area is vulnerable to injury.
- Different bones harden fully at different times. Bones are not fully mature until a person is around 18–21 years old. Up to this age bones are softer and more susceptible to injury.
- A young person's shape changes rapidly and they have to battle to adapt to changes in strength, weight ratio, balance and co-ordination.

Football involves the strong actions of running, jumping, landing, kicking and fast direction changes, which increase the chance of injury if excessively performed. Overuse injuries can often be dismissed as growing pains and medical diagnosis is not sought. This should never occur and football parents should be aware of overuse so that they do not dismiss any complaints from their child as being growing pains and nothing more serious.

The four regions of the body that are particularly affected in footballers are the back, knees, shins and ankles/heels.

Signs and symptoms

The following should serve as a guide. If several of the signs and symptoms are present, a medical opinion should be sought.

- Problems usually come on gradually and continue while the player continues to train and play.
- Main symptoms are aching, discomfort or pain in the area of the problem.
- There is pain when a particular movement is performed.
- There is no history of direct injury.
- The player may complain of stiffness/aching after or during training or competition.
- It may take several hours/days for the player to become pain free following training or a match.
- Your child may demonstrate tenderness to touch or pressure over the affected area.
- Visible swelling may be present in the case of an overuse injury affecting the knee or heel area.
- Your child shows a history of missing training sessions or matches due to injury.
- The problem does not go away. It will get progressively worse with continued activity.

Best Practice Never dismiss complaints of injury from your child, and use the above guide to decide whether to get them examined by a professional. If in doubt you should always seek medical advice. Don't bully your child by making them feel that they should be able to deal with any pain and therefore shouldn't complain – this may lead to them keeping quiet, so that you do not even become aware of a potential serious injury.

What to do

Pain, swelling, tenderness and aching are nature's way of informing us that something is wrong with our body. If some or all of the signs and symptoms previously outlined are present then a medical opinion should be sought.

Avoiding overuse – keeping it varied

It is extremely important to keep training varied in order to avoid overuse, this has been discussed in greater detail on page 102.

Best Practice Keeping training sessions varied and interesting will not only help young players to improve their chance of avoiding injury but should also assist their interest and motivation levels.

As all parents, teachers and coaches of young players will know, maintaining the interest of any young person is not an easy task and varied training sessions should assist in keeping up interest and concentration levels. Another book in this series *The Official FA Guide to Basic Team Coaching* looks at a variety of training sessions suitable for young players.

Is the first question you ask your child 'Did you win'? If so, ask yourself if you place too much emphasis on winning, and how this could affect your child and their participation in the game.

Don't let your emotions get the better of you and affect how you communicate to your child, coach or referee during a match. Your role as a parent is critical.

Very few young players will become international stars, so whilst you should encourage your child, also be realistic and manage their expectations.

Children of different ages have varying characteristics and this will affect why they play the game and when they develop certain skills.

At the end of every season only a few teams will be lucky enough to win a trophy so be realistic when talking about the team's prospects for glory!

To get the most out of young players, training sessions should be varied. Don't be afraid to speak to your child's coach if you feel that sessions are not as varied as they should be.

Keeping your eyes and ears open is an important factor in recognizing an overuse injury. In many instances, potential problems can be minimized by early recognition and prompt action. Remember never to dismiss signs and symptoms; the chances of an overuse injury being sustained in a young player's career are real.

Reasons why teenagers stop playing

1 Decrease in interest. In our mid to late teens we suddenly find other interests. Going out with friends, for example, may be of greater importance than playing football.

2 Lack of parental support. If you go to an under 12s game you will see lots of parents, but go to an under 16 match and it is likely that there will be far fewer.

3 Competitiveness. Football can lose its fun factor as greater emphasis is placed on winning at all costs.

4 Too much pressure. As we looked at earlier in the book, too much pressure on players often leads to them leaving the game.

5 Part-time jobs. Increasingly more teenagers have part-time weekend jobs that affect their ability to participate in training and matches especially now that we have a seven days per week work culture.

6 Shattered dreams. The realization that we are not the next David Beckham, Ronaldo or Mia Hamm.

7 Boredom. This might be as simple as the fact that the coach hasn't changed the coaching methods for years, or that the player never gets a regular place in the team and becomes fed up of making the effort.

8 Other pressures. For example, children having too much homework – an increased number of deadlines and a greater number of exams can mean that children are forced to give up personal interests.

9   Other available activities. Recently other sports such as golf
    and rugby have become more accessible. There are also, of
    course, other distractions such as computers, computer
    games, and television.

10 Peer pressure. Children are often influenced by their friends
    and what's popular and what's not. This is very likely to have
    an effect on what your child thinks, wears and does.

Moving into adult football

Statistic
70% of young people are not playing football by the age
of 21.

For many children the move from youth football to the adult game becomes a jump too far. Some of the possible reasons for this are:

- Physical strength. Some players may not be able to cope with the physical demands and physical strength of other teammates or the opposition.

- Lack of playing opportunity. The ability to break into the team becomes much tougher as a player becomes older and more experienced. In adult teams, the starting line-up is fairly rigid and players on the sidelines may find it difficult to become part of the starting 11. Whereas in youth football players only compete against players of a similar age, in adult football the age range is greater and therefore the potential for a larger pool of players increases making opportunities to play more difficult to come by.

- The more aggressive attitude in adult football. Older players will often have a different attitude to youth players with more focus on winning and the competitive aspects of the game and some younger players may find this difficult to deal with. Football is full of players that have failed to handle the more aggressive aspects of first-team/adult football particularly if players are rushed into action with senior teams too soon.

- Lack of confidence in mixing with adults. Children often find communicating with adults intimidating and may take a while to gain in confidence alongside often louder adult teammates. If younger players become part of the team and see the same players more often this should become less of an issue.

- Social aspects of adult football. So much of adult football is about the additional social elements of being part of a team that younger players may not be able to participate in due to their age (having a beer after the game).

Of course, all that said, many young people make the successful transition even at an early age into the adult game. Just look at players such as Michael Owen, Wayne Rooney, Ronaldo or even Pele.

▓ Look at the youth-to-adult transition within your child's club. Are there measures in place to ensure that the transition is as smooth as possible? Do the adult players support younger players that join their team from the youth team? Perhaps you can get involved in this and suggest implementing a structure that will help younger players to ensure that this doesn't become a reason for giving up.

Making it easier

There are ways to help children in coping with the transition to adult football. The following advice will help your child move from youth to adult football:

- Instead of a leap from the under 15s to adult football, encourage a smoother transition if possible. Try to ensure your child moves up the age groups and plays in the under 16 team then the under 18 team before joining the adults. Some leagues are beginning to offer an under 21 league as an additional stepping stone, so look at what is offered in your area.

- Ensure that the youth club supports the transition either into their own adult section or has an established relationship with local adult teams, where the coaches work together to ensure a smooth transition.

- Make sure that when choosing an adult team, you choose one that is right for your child. The same principles about choosing a club that we covered earlier in Chapter 3 apply here.

What you can do as a parent to help

- Be supportive. Make sure that you keep going to the games whenever possible. It may not seem to be so necessary as your child becomes older, but it is just as vital and will give your child the support that is essential if they are to continue playing the game. This will mean that you are able to talk about the game with them, and this will become a more sophisticated analysis and be more rewarding as your child develops and he/she gains a greater understanding of the game.

- Be available to help with the little things, even if it seems they are no longer as necessary as they were. Helping with transport, for example, will still be needed and much appreciated.

- Go to live games together or watch the televized ones as an alternative. Not only is this an enjoyable pastime, it also means that you can analyse the games together, discuss what is happening and what is good and bad football, and become students of the game, understanding each other's views and learning from one another.

- Encourage your child, but do not pressure them to stay involved. Let them make their own decisions and whilst you should maintain your support and encouragement, don't let this turn into making them feel pressurized, especially as they get older.

Summary

- **Recognize that your child has other interests and pressures on their time.**

- **Keep supporting your child and continue to take an interest.**

- **Look out for overuse injuries.**

- **Whilst there may be lots of reasons to stop playing, all of the benefits discussed in earlier chapters continue to be relevant.**

- **Help your child with the transition into adult football.**

Self testers

1 What are the four main causes of overuse injuries?

2 Name as many reasons as you can why children stop playing football.

3 What are the main reasons why children find it difficult to make the transition from youth to adult football?

Action plan

Think of five things that you can do to help maintain your child's interest in the game. Carry out these ideas and note which ones had the most effect. Continue to do them and show support to your child.

Conclusion

Being a football parent, just like being a parent, is a tremendous responsibility. It is an opportunity to help shape a young person and help develop a lifelong love of a great game.

So let's recap on some key points:

- Share your child's interest and be active in your child's development.
- Encourage your child to play the game but be careful not to pressurize him/her.
- Be realistic in what your child can achieve.
- Remember the benefits to your child's physical literacy and social development.
- Be careful when choosing a club – choose one that is most suitable for your child and remember to find the philosophy that is right for your child.
- All clubs need help, so think of how can you can help as a volunteer, and remember that every bit helps.
- Keep supporting your child. This is particularly important when things are not going well, so don't be critical – support them at all times.

- Remember to be positive – even if you are disappointed as your child will rely on you to remain positive about their football playing.

- Help your child to develop and learn and take into account the fact that we all learn differently.

- As a football parent you should set an example to your child and to other parents.

- Follow the football parent's code of conduct.

- Watch out for overuse injuries and don't dismiss small injuries – you may live to regret the consequences.

- Keep supporting your children when they become teenagers – keep sharing that interest.

- Help your child move from youth to adult football and recognize that there may be some difficulties.

- Many thousands of people have not only enjoyed being football parents, but have found that it has produced a new hobby for them, which has led to new friends and interests.

Having read the book, what are you going to do now?

Ask yourself the following:

1 What are you going to change?
2 How are you going to help your child?
3 What do you want to achieve in the next 12 months?

I hope you've enjoyed the book, but most importantly I hope that the book has provided you with advice and practical ideas to assist you and your child to get more enjoyment out of the great game that is football.

Appendix 1: Frequently asked questions

Question How many laws are there in football?

Answer It may surprise you but there are only 17 Laws:

1 The field of play (the pitch and goals)

2 The ball

3 The number of players

4 The players' equipment

5 The referee

6 The assistant referee

7 The duration of the match

8 The start and restart of play

9 When the ball is in or out of play

10 The method of scoring

11 Offside

12 Fouls and misconduct

13 Free kicks

14 The penalty kick

15 The throw-in

16 The goal kick

17 The corner kick

For a detailed introduction to The Laws of the Game see *The Official FA Guide to Basic Refereeing*.

Question So how many players are there in a team?

Answer   Football is usually played between teams of 11 per side. The minimum any team can have is seven players. In childrens football the laws are sometimes modified, with less numbers for example in seven-a-side, in England we call this Mini Soccer.

Lots of people also enjoy playing small sided football, this can be anything from three to seven a-side. We also have futsal, which is the FIFA recognized small game, which is for five-a-side.

Question So why play Mini Soccer?

Answer   Mini Soccer provides the best introduction to the worlds greatest game. Its smaller pitch, more appropriate sized goal and less players enables the player to have a greater involvement in the game.

Question When are you offside?

Answer   When the referee says so! No seriously, it is when a forward is closer to the opposition goal line than two of the opposing team when the ball is played forward by one of their own team, except if the player is in their own half of the field. To be offside, the player must be looking to gain an advantage or active in the play.

Question How long is a game?

Answer   In adult football they play 45 minutes each way. In youth and veterans they usually play reduced time – 35 or 40 minutes each way. For under 10s The FA have a rule, which states that a player must not play more than 60 minutes on any one day and 45 minutes for under 8s.

Question So what is a friendly?

Answer Some would have us believe a friendly game is not competitive . . . don't believe them – every time team A plays team B it's a competitive game! No, a friendly is a game with no points at stake and not in a cup competition.

Question What are the positions in football?

Answer **Goalkeeper** – is there to stop the other team from scoring a goal.

Defenders

Right back – will play on the right side of the defence.

Left back – as above, but on the left side of the defence (see it's simple!).

Central defender – defenders who are in the middle of the field.

Sweeper – usually plays just behind the defenders, their job is to 'sweep up' any mistakes.

Midfield

Right/Centre/Left midfield – to play in the middle of the team, linking defence and attack.

Wingbacks – this is usually when a team plays five in defence and the left and right wingbacks must not only defend but go forward – more than a right or left back would be expected to!

Wingers – on the right or left, their job is to get wide/on the touch line.

Forwards – attackers, creating chances, scoring goals – or as the defenders normally call them, 'glory grabbers!'

Now my favourite position, the one I had a long career with . . . substitute!

Question So what is a formation?

Answer   It is the way the coach/manager sets up their team. Here are some examples:

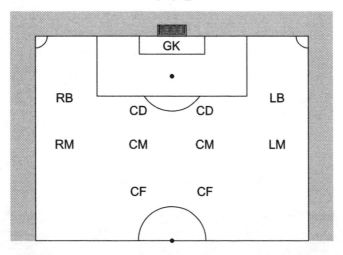

4–3–3

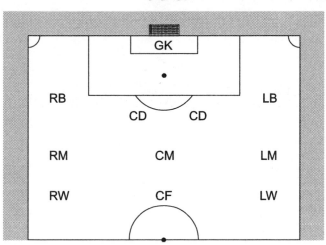

5–4–1

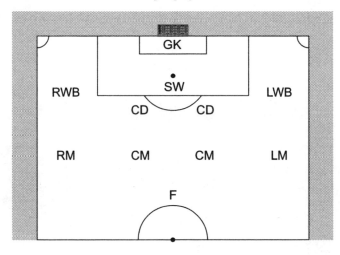

4–4–1–1

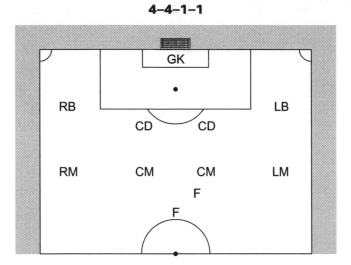

4–5–1

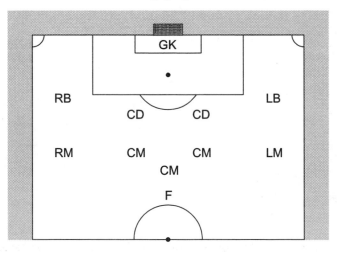

3–2–3–2

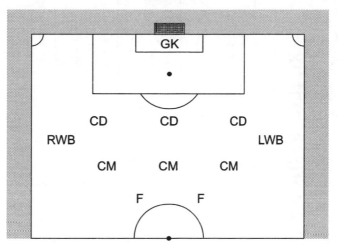

GK – Goalkeeper

RB – Right back

LB – Left back

CD – Central defender (centre half)

SW – Sweeper

RM – Right midfield

CM – Centre midfield

LM – Left midfield

RWB – Right wing back

LWB – Left wing back

RW – Right winger

LW – Left winger

F – Forward

Question On TV the commentators will describe a player as 'playing in the hole' – what does this mean?

Answer It is a player who plays in front of the midfield but behind the forwards.

Appendix 2: FA Learning coaching course matrix

Course	For Whom	Prerequisites	Where
Coaching Level 1	Coaches of young players.	Open entry course for anybody aged over 16 years of age. You don't need any experience, just an interest in the game and motivation to improve your knowledge.	Locally run courses managed by County FA's as well as residentially run courses at approved FA centres.
Coaching Level 2	Coaches with some experience at any level with regular participation.	Open entry course for anybody aged over 16 years of age with regular practical experience of participation of football.	Locally run courses managed by County FA's as well as residentially run courses at approved FA centres.
Coaching Level 3 /UEFA 'B'	Coaches that are working with a team over an extensive period.	Anybody over 18 years of age. Candidates must hold the Level 2 Coaching Certificate.	Locally run courses managed by County FA's as well as residentially run courses at approved FA centres.
UEFA 'A'	Coaches with experience at representative level.	Candidates must hold the Level 3 /UEFA 'B' Certificate in Coaching.	Nationally run course that takes place residentially at approved FA centres.

For more information and to enrol on a course visit www.TheFA.com/FALearning

Appendix 3: Code of Conduct

Football is the national game. All those involved with the game at every level and whether as a player, match official, coach, owner or administrator, have a responsibility, above and beyond compliance with the law, to act according to the highest standards of integrity, and to ensure that the reputation of the game is, and remains, high. This code applies to all those involved in football under the auspices of The Football Association.

Community

Football, at all levels, is a vital part of a community. Football will take into account community feeling when making decisions.

Equality

Football is opposed to discrimination of any form and will promote measures to prevent it, in whatever form, from being expressed.

Participants

Football recognizes the sense of ownership felt by those who participate at all levels of the game. This includes those who play, those who coach or help in any way, and those who officiate, as well as administrators and supporters. Football is committed to appropriate consultation.

Young people
Football acknowledges the extent of its influence over young people and pledges to set a positive example.

Propriety
Football acknowledgs that public confidence demands the highest standards of financial and administrative behavioiur within the game, and will not tolerate corruption or improper practices.

Trust and respect
Football will uphold a relationship of trust and respect between all involved in the game, whether they are individuals, clubs or other organizations.

Violence
Football rejects the use of violence of any nature by anyone involved in the game.

Fairness
Football is committed to fairness in its dealings with all involved in the game.

Integrity and fair play
Football is committed to the principle of playing to win, consistent with fair play.

Code of Conduct for coaches
Coaches are key to the establishment of ethics within football. Their concept of ethics and their attitude directly affects the behaviour of players under their supervision. Coaches are, therefore, expected to pay particular care to the moral aspect of their conduct.

Coaches have to be aware that almost all of their everyday decisions and choices of actions, as well as strategic targets, have ethical implications.

It is natural that winning constitutes a basic concern for coaches. This code is not intended to conflict with that. However, the code calls for coaches to disassociate themselves from a 'win-at-all-costs' attitude.

Increased responsibility is requested from coaches involved in coaching young people. The health, safety, welfare and moral education of young people are the first priority, before the achievement of the reputation of the club, school, coach or parent.

Set out below is the FA Coaches' Association Code of Conduct (which reflects the standards expressed by the National Coaching Foundation and the National Association of Sports Coaches), which forms the benchmark for all involved in coaching.

1 **Coaches must respect the rights, dignity and worth of each and every person and treat each equally within the context of the sport.**

2 **Coaches must place the well-being and safety of each player above all other considerations, including the development of performance.**

3 **Coaches must adhere to all guidelines laid down by governing bodies.**

4 **Coaches must develop an appropriate working relationship with each player based on mutual trust and respect.**

5 **Coaches must not exert undue influence to obtain personal benefit or reward.**

6 **Coaches must encourage and guide players to accept responsibility for their own behaviour and performance.**

7 **Coaches must ensure that the activities they direct or advocate are appropriate for the age, maturity, experience and ability of players.**

8 Coaches should, at the outset, clarify with the players (and, where appropriate, parent) exactly what is expected of them and also what they are entitled to expect from their coach.

9 Coaches must co-operate fully with other specialists (e.g. other coaches, officials, sports scientists, doctors, physiotherapists) in the best interests of the player.

10 Coaches must always promote the positive aspects of the sport (e.g. fair play) and never condone violations of the Laws of the Game, behaviour contrary to the spirit of the Laws of the Game or relevant rules and regulations or the use of prohibited substances or techniques.

11 Coaches must consistently display high standards of behaviour and appearance.

12 Not to use or tolerate inappropriate language.

Code of Conduct for players

Players are the most important people in the sport. Playing for the team, and for the team to win, is the most fundamental part of the game. But winning at any cost is not the idea – fair play and respect for all others in the game is fundamentally important.

This Code is focused on players involved in top-class football. Nevertheless, the key concepts in the Code are valid for players at all levels.

Obligations towards the game

A player should:

1 Make every effort to develop their own sporting abilities, in terms of skill, technique, tactics and stamina.

2 Give maximum effort and strive for the best possible performance during a game, even if his/her team is in a psoition where the desired result has already been achieved.

3 Set a positive example for others, particularly young players and supporters.

4   Avoid all forms of gamesmanship and time-wasting.

5   Always have regard to the best interests of the game, including where publicly expressing an opinion on the game and any particular aspect of it, including others involved in the game.

6   Not use inappropriate language.

Obligations towards one's own team

A player should:

1   Make every effort consistent with fair play and the Laws of the Game to help his/her own team win.

2   Resist any influence which might, or might be seen to, bring into question his/her commitment to the team winning.

Respect for the Laws of the Game and competition rules

A player should:

1   Know and abide by the Laws, rules and spirit of the game, and the competition rules.

2   Accept success and failure, victory and defeat, equally.

3   Resist any temptation to take banned substances or use banned techniques.

Respect towards opponents

A player should:

1   Treat opponents with due respect at all times, irrespective of the result of the game.

2   Safeguard the physical fitness of opponents, avoid violence and rough play, and help injured opponents.

Respect towards the match officials

A player should:

1   Accept the decision of the match official without protest.

2   Avoid words or actions which may mislead a match official.

3   Show due respect towards match officials.

Respect towards team officials

A player should:

1   Abide by the instructions of their coach and team officials, provided they do not contradict the spirit of this Code.

2   Show due respect towards the team officials of the opposition.

Obligations towards the supporters

A player should:

1   Show due respect to the interests of the supporters.

Code of Conduct for team officials

This Code applies to all team/club officials (although some items may not apply to all officials).

Obligations towards the game

The team official should:

1   Set a positive example for others, particularly young players and supporters.

2   Promote and develop his/her own team having regard for the interest of the players, supporters and reputation of the national game.

3   Share knowledge and experience when invited to do so, taking into account the interest of the body that has requested this rather than personal interests.

4   Avoid all forms of gamesmanship.

5   Show due respect to match officials and others involved in the game.

6   Always have regard for the best interests of the game, including where publicly expressing an opinion of the game and any particular aspect of it, including others involved in the game.

7   Not use or tolerate inappropriate language.

Obligations towards the team

The Team Official should:

1 Make every effort to develop the sporting, technical and tactical levels of the club/team, and to obtain the best results by the team, using all permitted means.

2 Give priority to the interests of the team over individual interests.

3 Resist all illegal or unsporting influences, including banned substances and techniques.

4 Promote ethical principles.

5 Show due respect to the interests of players, coaches and other officials, at their own club/team and others.

Obligations towards the supporters

The Team Offical should:

1 Show due respect to the interests of supporters.

Respect towards the Match Officials

The Team Official should:

1 Accept the decisions of the Match Official without protest.

2 Avoid words or actions which may mislead a Match Official.

3 Show due respect towards Match Officials.

Code of Conduct for parents/spectators

Parents and spectators have a great influence on children's enjoyment and success in football. All children play football because they first and foremost love the game – it's fun. Remember that however good a child becomes at football within your club, it is important to reinforce the message to parents/spectators that positive encouragement will contribute to:

• Children enjoying football.

• A sense of personal achievement.

- **Self-esteem.**
- **Helping to improve the child's skill and techniques.**

A parent's/spectator's expectations and attitudes have a significant bearing on a child's attitude towards:

- **Other players.**
- **Officials.**
- **Managers.**
- **Spectators.**

Ensure that parents/spectators within your club are always positive and show encouragement towards all of the children, not just their own.

Encourage parents/spectators to:

- **Applaud the opposition as well as your own team.**
- **Avoid coaching the child during the game.**
- **Avoid shouting and screaming.**
- **Respect the referee's decision.**
- **Give attention to each of the children involved in football, not just the most talented.**
- **Give encouragement to everyone to participate in football.**

Ensure that the parents/spectators within your club agree and adhere to your club's Code of Conduct and Child Protection policy.

Appendix 4: Goalpost safety guidelines

The FA, along with the Department for Culture, Media and Sport, the Health and Safety Executive and the British Standards Institution (BSI), would like to draw your attention to the following guidelines for the safe use of goalposts.

Too many serious injuries and fatalities have occurred in recent years as a result of unsafe or incorrect use of goalposts. Safety is always of paramount importance and everyone in football must play their part to prevent similar incidents occurring in the future.

- **For safety reasons, goalposts of any size (including those which are portable and not installed permanently at a pitch or practice field) must always be anchored securely to the ground.**

  - **Portable goalposts must be secured by the use of chain anchors or appropriate anchor weights to prevent them from toppling forward.**

  - **It is essential that under no circumstances should children or adults be allowed to climb, swing or play on the structures of the goalposts.**

- Particular attention is drawn to the fact that, if not properly assembled and secured, portable goalposts may topple over.

- Regular inspections of goalposts should be carried out to check that they are properly maintained.

- Portable goalposts should not be left in place after use. They should be dismantled and removed to a place of secure storage.

- It is strongly recommended that nets should only be secured by plastic hooks or tape and not by metal cup hooks. Any metal cup hooks should, if possible, be removed and replaced. New goalposts should not be purchased if they include metal cup hooks that cannot be replaced.

- Goalposts that are homemade or have been altered from their original size or construction should not be used. These have been the cause of a number of deaths and injuries.

- Guidelines to prevent toppling:

  - Follow manufacturer's guidelines in assembling goalposts.

  - Before use, adults should:

    - Ensure each goal is anchored securely in its place.

    - Exert a significant downward force on the crossbar.

    - Exert a significant backward force on both upright posts.

    - Exert a significant forward force on both upright posts.

These actions must be repeated until it is established that the structure is secure. If not, alternative goals/pitches must be used.

For reference, you should note that The FA and BSI have developed a standard for future purchases (PAS 36:2000) available from BSI. It is hoped that this will be developed into a full British Standard in due course.

Contacts

**Fédération Internationale de
Football Association (FIFA)**
FIFA House
Hitzigweg 11
PO Box 85
8030 Zurich
Switzerland
Tel: +41-43/222 7777
Fax: +41-43/222 7878
Internet: http://www.fifa.com

Confederations

Asian Football Confederation (AFC)
AFC House, Jalan 1/155B
Bukit Jalil
Kuala Lumpur 57000
Malaysia
Tel: +60-3/8994 3388
Fax: +60-3/8994 2689
Internet: http://www.footballasia.com

**Confédération Africaine de
Football (CAF)**
3 Abdel Khalek Sarwat Street
El Hay El Motamayez
PO Box 23
6th October City
Egypt
Tel: +20-2/837 1000
Fax: +20-2/837 0006
Internet: http://www.cafonline.com

**Confederation of North, Central
American and Caribbean
Association Football
(CONCACAF)**
Central American and Caribbean
Association Football
725 Fifth Avenue, 17th Floor
New York, NY 10022
USA
Tel: +1-212/308 0044
Fax: +1-212/308 1851
Internet: http://www.concacaf.net

Confederación Sudamericana de Fútbol (CONMEBOL)
Autopista Aeropuerto Internacional y
Leonismo Luqueño
Luque (Gran Asunción)
Paraguay
Tel: +595-21/645 781
Fax: +595-21/645 791
Internet: http://www.conmebol.com

Oceania Football Confederation (OFC)
Ericsson Stadium
12 Maurice Road
PO Box 62 586
Penrose
Auckland
New Zealand
Tel: +64-9/525 8161
Fax: +64-9/525 8164
Internet: http://www.oceaniafootball
.com

Union European Football Association (UEFA)
Route de Genève 46
Nyon 1260
Switzerland
Tel: +41-22/994 4444
Fax: +41-22/994 4488
Internet: http://www.uefa.com

Associations

Argentina
Asociación del Fútbol Argentino (AFA)
Viamonte 1366/76
Buenos Aires 1053
Tel: ++54-11/4372 7900
Fax: ++54-11/4375 4410
Internet: http://www.afa.org.ar

Australia
Soccer Australia Limited (ASF)
Level 3
East Stand, Stadium Australia
Edwin Flack Avenue
Homebush NSW 2127
Tel: ++61-2/9739 5555
Fax: ++61-2/9739 5590
Internet: http://www.socceraustralia
.com.au

Belgium
Union Royale Belge des Sociétés de Football Assocation (URBSFA/KBV)
145 Avenue Houba de Strooper
Bruxelles 1020
Tel: ++32-2/477 1211
Fax: ++32-2/478 2391
Internet: http://www.footbel.com

Brazil
Confederação Brasileira de Futebol (CBF)
Rua Victor Civita 66
Bloco 1 – Edifício 5 – 5 Andar
Barra da Tijuca
Rio de Janeiro 22775-040
Tel: ++55-21/3870 3610
Fax: ++55-21/3870 3612
Internet: http://www.cbfnews.com

Cameroon
Fédération Camerounaise de Football (FECAFOOT)
Case postale 1116
Yaoundé
Tel: ++237/221 0012
Fax: ++237/221 6662
Internet: http://www.cameroon.fifa.com

Canada

The Canadian Soccer Association (CSA)
Place Soccer Canada
237 Metcalfe Street
Ottawa ONT K2P 1R2
Tel: ++1-613/237 7678
Fax: ++1-613/237 1516
Internet: http://www.canadasoccer.com

Costa Rica

Federación Costarricense de Fútbol (FEDEFUTBOL)
Costado Norte Estatua León Cortés
San José 670-1000
Tel: ++506/222 1544
Fax: ++506/255 2674
Internet: http://www.fedefutbol.com

Croatia

Croatian Football Federation (HNS)
Rusanova 13
Zagreb 10 000
Tel: ++385-1/236 1555
Fax: ++385-1/244 1501
Internet: http://www.hns-cff.hr

Czech Republic

Football Association of Czech Republic (CMFS)
Diskarska 100
Praha 6 16017
Tel: ++420-2/3302 9111
Fax: ++420-2/3335 3107
Internet: http://www.fotbal.cz

Denmark

Danish Football Association (DBU)
Idrættens Hus
Brøndby Stadion 20
Brøndby 2605
Tel: ++45-43/262 222
Fax: ++45-43/262 245
Internet: http://www.dbu.dk

England

The Football Association (The FA)
25 Soho Square
London W1D 4FA
Tel: ++44-207/745 4545
Fax: ++44-207/745 4546
Internet: http://www.TheFA.com

Finland

Suomen Palloliitto (SPL/FBF)
Urheilukatu 5
PO Box 191
Helsinki 00251
Tel: ++358-9/7421 51
Fax: ++358-9/7421 5200
Internet: http://www.palloliitto.fi

France

Fédération Française de Football (FFF)
60 Bis Avenue d'Iéna
Paris 75116
Tel: ++33-1/4431 7300
Fax: ++33-1/4720 8296
Internet: http://www.fff.fr

Germany

Deutscher Fussball-Bund (DFB)
Otto-Fleck-Schneise 6
Postfach 71 02 65
Frankfurt Am Main 60492
Tel: ++49-69/678 80
Fax: ++49-69/678 8266
Internet: http://www.dfb.de

Greece

Hellenic Football Federation (HFF)
137 Singrou Avenue
Nea Smirni
Athens 17121
Tel: ++30-210/930 6000
Fax: ++30-210/935 9666
Internet: http://www.epo.gr

Ireland Republic
The Football Association of Ireland (FAI)
80 Merrion Square, South
Dublin 2
Tel: ++353-1/676 6864
Fax: ++353-1/661 0931
Internet: http://www.fai.ie

Italy
Federazione Italiana Giuoco Calcio (FIGC)
Via Gregorio Allegri, 14
Roma 00198
Tel: ++39-06/84 911
Fax: ++39-06/84 912 526
Internet: http://www.figc.it

Japan
Japan Football Association (JFA)
JFA House
3-10-15, Hongo
Bunkyo-ku
Tokyo 113-0033
Tel: ++81-3/3830 2004
Fax: ++81-3/3830 2005
Internet: http://www.jfa.or.jp

Kenya
Kenya Football Federation (KFF)
PO Box 40234
Nairobi
Tel: ++254-2/608 422
Fax: ++254-2/249 855
Email: kff@todays.co.ke

Korea Republic
Korea Football Association (KFA)
1-131 Sinmunno, 2-ga
Jongno-Gu
Seoul 110-062
Tel: ++82-2/733 6764
Fax: ++82-2/735 2755
Internet: http://www.kfa.or.kr

Mexico
Federación Mexicana de Fútbol Asociación, A.C. (FMF)
Colima No. 373
Colonia Roma
Mexico, D.F. 06700
Tel: ++52-55/5241 0190
Fax: ++52-55/5241 0191
Internet: http://www.femexfut.org.mx

Netherlands
Koninklijke Nederlandse Voetbalbond (KNVB)
Woudenbergseweg 56–58
PO Box 515
Am Zeist 3700 AM
Tel: ++31-343/499 201
Fax: ++31-343/499 189
Internet: http://www.knvb.nl

Nigeria
Nigeria Football Association (NFA)
Plot 2033, Olusegun
Obasanjo Way, Zone 7, Wuse Abuja
PO Box 5101 Garki
Abuja
Tel: ++234-9/523 7326
Fax: ++234-9/523 7327
Email: nfa@microaccess.com

Northern Ireland
Irish Football Association Ltd. (IFA)
20 Windsor Avenue
Belfast BT9 6EE
Tel: ++44-28/9066 9458
Fax: ++44-28/9066 7620
Internet: http://www.irishfa.com

Paraguay
Asociación Paraguaya de Fútbol (APF)
Estadio de los Defensores del Chaco
Calle Mayor Martinez 1393
Asunción
Tel: ++595-21/480 120
Fax: ++595-21/480 124
Internet: http://www.apf.org.py

Poland
Polish Football Association (PZPN)
Polski Zwiazek Pilki Noznej
Miodowa 1
Warsaw 00-080
Tel: ++48-22/827 0914
Fax: ++48-22/827 0704
Internet: http://www.pzpn.pl

Portugal
Federação Portuguesa de Futebol (FPF)
Praça de Alegria, N. 25
PO Box 21.100
Lisbon 1250-004
Tel: ++351-21/325 2700
Fax: ++351-21/325 2780
Internet: http://www.fpf.pt

Romania
Romanian Football Federation (FRF)
House of Football
Str. Serg. Serbanica Vasile 12
Bucharest 73412
Tel: ++40-21/325 0678
Fax: ++40-21/325 0679
Internet: http://www.frf.ro

Russia
Football Union of Russia (RFU)
8 Luzhnetskaya Naberezhnaja
Moscow 119 992
Tel: ++7-095/201 1637
Fax: ++7-502/220 2037
Internet: http://www.rfs.ru

Scotland
The Scottish Football Association (SFA)
Hampden Park
Glasgow G42 9AY
Tel: ++44-141/616 6000
Fax: ++44-141/616 6001
Internet: http://www.scottishfa.co.uk

South Africa
South African Football Association (SAFA)
First National Bank Stadium
PO Box 910
Johannesburg 2000
Tel: ++27-11/494 3522
Fax: ++27-11/494 3013
Internet: http://www.safa.net

Spain

Real Federación Española de Fútbol (RFEF)
Ramon y Cajal, s/n
Apartado postale 385
Madrid 28230
Tel: ++34-91/495 9800
Fax: ++34-91/495 9801
Internet: http://www.rfef.es

Sweden

Svenska Fotbollförbundet (SVFF)
PO Box 1216
Solna 17 123
Tel: ++46-8/735 0900
Fax: ++46-8/735 0901
Internet: http://www.svenskfotboll.se

Switzerland

Schweizerischer Fussball-Verband (SFV/ASF)
Postfach
Bern 15 3000
Tel: ++41-31/950 8111
Fax: ++41-31/950 8181
Internet: http://www.football.ch

Tunisia

Fédération Tunisienne de Football (FTF)
Maison des Fédérations Sportives
Cité Olympique
Tunis 1003
Tel: ++216-71/233 303
Fax: ++216-71/767 929
Internet: http://www.ftf.org.tn

Turkey

Türkiye Futbol Federasyonu (TFF)
Konaklar Mah. Ihlamurlu Sok. 9
4. Levent
Istanbul 80620
Tel: ++90-212/282 7020
Fax: ++90-212/282 7015
Internet: http://www.tff.org

United States of America

US Soccer Federation (USSF)
US Soccer House
1801 S. Prairie Avenue
Chicago IL 60616
Tel: ++1-312/808 1300
Fax: ++1-312/808 1301
Internet: http://www.ussoccer.com

Uruguay

Asociación Uruguaya de Fútbol (AUF)
Guayabo 1531
Montevideo 11200
Tel: ++59-82/400 4814
Fax: ++59-82/409 0550
Internet: http://www.auf.org.uy

Wales

The Football Association of Wales, Ltd (FAW)
Plymouth Chambers
3 Westgate Street
Cardiff CF10 1DP
Tel: ++44-29/2037 2325
Fax: ++44-29/2034 3961
Internet: http://www.faw.org.uk

For details of County FAs please see **www.TheFA.com**/Grassroots

LEARNING

Index

All about FA Learning

FA Learning is the Educational Division of The FA and is responsible for the delivery, co-ordination and promotion of its extensive range of educational products and services. This includes all courses and resources for coaching, refereeing, psychology, sports science, medical exercise, child protection, crowd safety and teacher training.

The diverse interests of those involved in football ensures that FA Learning remains committed to providing resources and activities suitable for all individuals whatever their interests, experience or level of expertise.

Whether you're a Premier League Manager, sports psychologist or interested parent, our aim is to have courses and resources available that will improve your knowledge and understanding.

If you've enjoyed reading this book and found the content useful then why not take a look at FA Learning's website to find out the types of courses and additional resources available to help you continue your football development.

The website contains information on all the national courses and events managed by The FA as well as information on a number of online resources:

- **Psychology for Soccer Level 1 – Our first online qualification.**
- **Soccer Star – Free online coaching tool for young players.**
- **Soccer Parent – Free online course for parents.**

All these resources can be accessed at home from your own PC and are currently used by thousands of people across the world.

Psychology for Soccer Level 1

Enrol today and join hundreds of others around the world taking part in FA Learning's first ever online qualification.

This pioneering project is the first of its kind to be provided by any Football Governing Body and is available to anyone with access to the internet. There are no additional qualifications required to take part other than an interest in learning more about the needs of young players and an email address!

The course is aimed at coaches, parents and teachers of 7–12 year olds looking to gain an introduction to psychology and features modules based on 'true to life' player, coach and parent scenarios.

Psychology for Soccer Level 1 is a completely interactive, multimedia learning experience. Don't just take our word for it, read some of the comments from those that have already completed the course:

'Wow what a wonderful course! Thank you for the time and effort to make this possible.' **Tracy Scott**

'Just passed the final assessment ... it was a good experience to learn this way and hopefully more qualifications will become available in this format. Thanks.' **Shayne Hall**

'I am a professional football coach working in schools and clubs and have travelled all around the world. I have really enjoyed the literature in this course and it has made me think about how I should address my coaching sessions. I want to progress in the field of sport psychology and this course has whetted my appetite for this subject.' **Chris Rafael Sabater**

The course modules are:

- Psychology and Soccer
- Motivation
- Learning and Acquiring skills
- Psychological Development
- Environment and Social Influences

In addition to the five course modules, learners also have access to a number of further benefits included as part of the course fee. The benefits include:

- Three months support from qualified FA tutors
- Classroom specific online discussion forums
- A global online discussion forum
- All successful students receive a FA Qualification in psychology

- An exclusive resource area containing over 100 articles and web links relating to coaching 7–12 year olds.

Within the five modules, there are over 20 sessions totaling over eight hours worth of content. Including the use of discussion forums, resource area and the course tasks, we anticipate the course will take on average 20 hours to complete.

For more information and to enroll on the course visit
www.**TheFA.com**/FALearning.

THE OFFICIAL FA GUIDE TO
FITNESS FOR FOOTBALL

Be a part of the game

The Official FA Guide to Fitness for Football provides essential knowledge and advice for everyone who plays the game.

This book includes:
- **basic physiology and nutrition**
- **training strategies**
- **the physiological differences between adults and children.**

Packed with practical exercises, information and expert advice, this book will improve your understanding and enhance your ability and enjoyment of the world's greatest game.

The author, **Dr Richard Hawkins**, is the Deputy Head of Exercise Science at The Football Association.

FA Learning
'learning through football'

TheFA.com/FALearning

Visit the website for information on all FA Learning's educational activities.

LEARNING

THE OFFICIAL FA GUIDE TO
RUNNING A CLUB

Be a part of the game

The Official FA Guide to Running a Club is written for anyone involved in the administration side of the game.

This book includes:
- **advice on how to start and run a club**
- **who to turn to for help**
- **how to deal with any problems that may occur**
- **finance, administration, PR and marketing.**

Packed with practical exercises, information and expert advice, this book will improve your understanding and enhance your ability and enjoyment of the world's greatest game.

The author, **Les Howie**, is responsible for the development of all clubs in the non-professional national game for The Football Association

FA Learning
'learning through football'

TheFA.com/FALearning

Visit the website for information on all FA Learning's educational activities.

THE OFFICIAL FA GUIDE TO
PSYCHOLOGY FOR FOOTBALL

Be a part of the game

The Official FA Guide to Psychology for Football is an introductory guide for anyone who wants to understand the needs of young players.

This book includes:
- **understanding the motivation, learning and development of players**
- **the affect of a player's environment**
- **how to develop individual strategies.**

Packed with practical exercises, information and expert advice, this book will improve your understanding and enhance your ability and enjoyment of the world's greatest game.

The author, **Dr Andy Cale**, is The Football Association's Education Advisor and was previously a lecturer in Sports Psychology at Loughborough University.

FA Learning
'learning through football'

TheFA.com/FALearning

Visit the website for information on all FA Learning's educational activities.

LEARNING

THE OFFICIAL FA GUIDE TO
BASIC TEAM COACHING

Be a part of the game

The Official FA Guide to Basic Team Coaching covers all the
essential aspects of coaching and is vital for those who coach
amateur football, or who are considering becoming a coach.

This book includes:
- **team strategies and tactics**
- **leadership and management**
- **match analysis.**

Packed with practical exercises, information and expert advice,
this book will improve your understanding and enhance your
ability and enjoyment of the world's greatest game.

The author, **Les Reed**, is The FA's Acting Technical Director and
was formerly the Assistant Manager at Charlton Athletic. Les has
coached England players at every level from youth to senior teams.

FA Learning
'learning through football'

TheFA.com/FALearning

Visit the website for information on all FA
Learning's educational activities.